Entrepreneur
VOICES

ON

COMPANY CULTURE

The Staff of Entrepreneur Media, Inc.

Entrepreneur
PRESS

Entrepreneur Press, Publisher
Cover Design: Andrew Welyczko
Production and Composition: Eliot House Productions

This publication is designed to provide accurate and
authoritative information in regard to the subject matter covered.
It is sold with the understanding that the publisher is not
engaged in rendering legal, accounting or other professional
services. If legal advice or other expert assistance is required, the
services of a competent professional person should be sought.

Library of Congress Cataloging-in-Publication Data
  Names: Lewis, Derek, author. | Entrepreneur Media, Inc.,
    author.
  Title: Entrepreneur voices on company culture / by the Staff
    of Entrepreneur Media, Inc.
  Description: Irvine, Calif.: Entrepreneur Media, Inc., [2018]
  Identifiers: LCCN 2017058402 | ISBN 978-1-59918-626-9 (alk.
    paper) | ISBN 1-59918-626-8 (alk. paper)
  Subjects: LCSH: Corporate culture.
  Classification: LCC HD58.7 .E446 2018 | DDC 658.3/01—dc23
  LC record available at https://lccn.loc.gov/2017058402

Printed in the United States of America
22 21 20 19   10 9 8 7 6 5 4 3 2 1

CONTENTS

PART II
LEADING

Contents

Contents

FOREWORD BY JASON FEIFER

Editor-in-Chief, Entrepreneur magazine

"Why do you like working here?"
As the editor in chief of *Entrepreneur*, overseeing a staff of journalists and producers, it's not a question I'd ever flat-out ask someone on my team. Just imagine the awkwardness of that—the manager fishing for compliments, the employee scrambling to say whatever they think the manager wants to hear. But any manager can hear employees answering that question on their

own. It happens in beautiful, unexpected moments. Maybe in a meeting. Maybe in office kitchen chit-chat. Maybe, frankly, at the nearby bar over happy hour. Colleagues will start trading notes about their past work experiences, and will soon circle back to their current, shared experience. What's successful here, they'll ask? What's not?

Listen closely in those moments. If you've built your company's culture the right way, you'll already know the answers to those questions.

Company culture is a hard phrase to define. It's an abstraction—not some specific set of policies or a blueprint you can overlay on any organization. Rather, it's a collection of things large and small. It's a sum of parts: of how employees are treated, of how they treat each other, of what support they find at work, of what day-to-day life is like for them, and what produces their greatest sources of enjoyment and pride. It's often said that there is no right or wrong culture; there's only a culture that works, or a culture that doesn't. It starts with a leader, but must filter completely downward. Company culture requires cohesion. Everyone must buy in.

At some level, you of course know this. You wouldn't have picked this book up without it. You understand that companies live and die by their culture. It may not be as tangible or even as visible as the product you make or the revenue numbers you flaunt, but culture is the foundation upon which all the rest is built. And yet, you aren't alone in wondering how to improve your own company's culture. It's not an easy, straightforward, or simple task. The answer is different for everyone.

That's why we've structured this book the way that we have. There are no one-size-fits-all guides to company culture; that would be literally impossible to write. Rather, this book is a collection—of essays, of ideas, of conversations, of experiments, of insights, of the absolute best and most useful thoughts we found from people who truly understand how to build culture the right way. By understanding the experiences and insights contained in these pages, you'll develop the instincts to shape your own culture.

So, back to that question: "Why do you like working here?" Recently, I had one of those wonderful moments where my team started answering the question. It happened while some editors and I were sitting around talking about the state of our industry. Media folks do that a lot these days; it's a wild and uncertain time. And soon, inevitably, the conversation turned to our own jobs, and our own experiences.

Foreword by Jason Feifer

One editor said he liked how small our team was—that everyone's role felt extremely well-defined, and that, as a result, we all trusted and knew exactly how to work with each other. Another said she appreciated how supportive we are of side projects—that this is a place that expects hard work, but that also respects ambition and supports its employees' growth. Another liked how flexible we are about time; we trust that everyone meets deadlines, so we're not especially concerned about where any one team member is at any one time.

This was all gratifying to hear, because it was exactly what I wanted my team to experience. It is, frankly, an extension of my own vision of the perfect office: A tight, self-motivated superstar team, with each member eager to kick butt because they feel fulfilled by their work while never feeling trapped by it. And it was also a self-fulfilling vision: I hire people who I know share these values, and who approach work the way I do. I've always had side projects throughout my career, for example. They've helped me widen my skillsets, and I'd inevitably plow those skills back into my full-time gig. I wanted team members who did the same.

Can I continue to improve our culture? Of course. And I want to always be mindful of that. But I tell you this story as a way to say: I had a vision and found people who shared that vision, and as a result, the culture I wanted filtered through my team. It starts with the leader. It starts with you. And this book is your starting point. What comes next is the fun part.

CULTURE IS YOUR EDGE

While you might think of company culture in terms of morale, productivity, and success, it's important to consider the deeper, potentially life-changing aspects of culture, too. Your company's culture is not just about what you do—it's also about what you allow. What's acceptable? What's unacceptable? What's *completely* unacceptable? How do you create a culture that honors your company's mission as well as the people who help foster that vision every day?

Your answers to those questions not only determine the course of your company's future, but they affect the life of every stakeholder in your company, from your investors to your employees' loved ones to the person who swaps out the jug on your water cooler.

As the interview with the founder of WP Engine points out, you already have a company culture—the only question is whether you're intentional about it. Surely, no entrepreneur has said, "I want to start a company where we hurt people and degrade their sense of self-worth—where our employees hate to come to work and where we scam our customers and vendors. *That's* the kind of business I envision."

Quite the opposite: many entrepreneurs went off on their own specifically because they hated their employer's way of doing business. They wanted to build a wonderful company where people love to work. Most entrepreneurs truly want to create more than just an amazing product—they want to create an amazing company.

The great thing about being an entrepreneur is that you're in charge. It doesn't matter what stage of the game you're in, from simply having an idea to being a solopreneur to managing scores of employees: as the founder, owner, and chief bottle washer, you get to say what flies and what doesn't . . . unlike, say, the CEO of a decades-old global behemoth.

Unfortunately, "culture" is often an afterthought. It often happens by accident, with little thought as to how it's shaping up until "the way it's always been done around here" becomes so entrenched that changing anything is like turning the *Titanic* around. But it's never too early to start—literally. In fact, the best time to get crystal clear on your vision for your company's culture is before you ever start your business. The second best time is right now.

The companies we know best know that growing a great culture is a work in progress. United Airlines can't change its culture to copy Southwest Airlines' success and results. Herb Kelleher started shaping the airline's unique approach to business when Southwest had only two routes: Dallas-Houston and Dallas-San Antonio. Because the company did such a great job infusing the company's spirit into its early years, it's taken on a life of its own.

You'll note the same spirit in the interview with Todd Graves, the founder of Raising Cane's, now the fastest growing restaurant chain in the U.S. Even when the "company" was just Todd and a handful of part-time college students serving chicken fingers to other college students, he knew how he wanted his restaurant to feel, how he wanted his employees to feel, and how he wanted his customers to feel. The moral of his story is: it's never too early.

But wherever you find yourself in your entrepreneurial journey, you don't have to go it alone. What you're about to read represents some of the best articles from *Entrepreneur*. In short, these are the best of the best.

Our team of writers helps you navigate the ever-changing world of company culture from how to attract and keep great employees and build morale to taking your in-house culture to the broader community through great outreach. For example, we address the tokens of superficial workplace culture, often using ping pong tables as a prime example of something decidedly not representative of what culture truly is—to the point that we had edit out at least half of the references to keep the repetition at a manageable level. Apparently, we are either sick of ping pong tables or sick of hearing about them. Maybe both.

You're going to read about the time an entire company's staff that quit all on the same day, leaving the owner to pick up the pieces. The story of the restaurant with a "best butt" award will surely stick with you for years to come. Perhaps most poignant is the last section of the book that deals with what to do if, like many entrepreneurs, you look up one day and find that you have a dysfunctional culture. What do you do?

You see, this book isn't about how to copy the vibe of some cool tech startup. We focus on the things that matter—the cultural elements that result in not just great places to work and great balance sheets to boot, but that create a better environment and support a better life for everyone involved. We are serious about doing good while doing well. A great company culture is not just a nice thing to have, but an essential factor in the success of companies going forward. Companies without a strong sense of purpose and direction will be left behind by those whose people love to come to work, whose customers love to work with them, and whose leaders can't wait to get to work in the morning.

This isn't a book about culture—it's about the future of how we do business.

CLARITY

As you're about to read, we now have solid data to back up what great entrepreneurs have intuitively known for years: companies that are great to work for outperform their competitors whose employees dislike showing up for work. That's on virtually every quantifiable measure—from productivity to bottom-line revenues.

But the best places to work for didn't arrive there by accident.

Those companies' cultures were deliberate. The founders and leaders found clarity about what was important, what was trivial, what was non-negotiable, and what was necessary.

We kick off this section with two chapters that represent what much of this entire book is about. Chapter 1 dispels the idea that "workplace culture" necessitates a literal workplace; and that company culture is about the people, not the place. Chapter 2 puts two companies side-by-side that, on paper, should be identical . . . yet are diametric opposites solely because of the culture their founders set in the beginning.

This first section packs a serious punch with inspiration, hope, and insightful expert interviews. By the time you're finished, there shouldn't be a doubt in your mind on the absolute necessity of having a clear vision, communicating that vision, living that vision, and reaping the rewards of that vision.

1

CREATING ONE OF THE BEST WORK CULTURES IN AMERICA ... WITH ZERO OFFICES

Sara Sutton Fell

In February 2017, *Entrepreneur* and Culture IQ released their second annual list of the Top Company Cultures in America, featuring 153 companies with "high-performance cultures." For the second year in a row, a company with a completely remote workforce is included on the list: FlexJobs.

As the founder and CEO of FlexJobs, I can tell you that, while this is an honor, the distinction is particularly appreciated because many people think that a remote company can't even have a company culture, let alone a great one.

It takes a conscientious effort and continuous dedication to build an organization that actively supports workers to do their best work and be their best selves. All the companies on this list believe a thriving company culture can fuel the fire of a growing business and result in a better bottom line.

The inclusion of FlexJobs on the Top Company Cultures list highlights that it's possible to have a remote company with a fantastic company culture. Furthermore, it points to the idea that remote work can even enhance and benefit company cultures.

Entrepreneur and Culture IQ focused on "Ten Core Qualities of Culture":

1. collaboration
2. innovation
3. agility
4. communication
5. support
6. wellness
7. mission and value alignment
8. work environment
9. responsibility
10. performance focus

Remote work is well-suited to support each of these qualities. Addressing all of these qualities let me share how we built one of the best company cultures in America at FlexJobs.

Agility, Performance Focus, and Mission-Value Alignment

We are a mission-driven organization: to help professionals find jobs that fit their lives with such options as flexible scheduling and the ability to work remotely. The fact that all of our own workers are remote means that our very way of working aligns with the mission and values of our company.

Remote work often strips away facetime and office politics. This naturally leads to a culture that focuses on results as our main performance measure. When and where people do their work isn't usually important; how, why, and what is.

And of course, we use remote work to find the best talent. Hiring someone based mainly on their skills and their fit with our company culture, rather than location, ensures that performance is a vital factor in recruitment and retention.

Work Environment, Support, and Wellness

Flexible work environments allow companies to better support their workers, especially when it comes to wellness. A flexible work environment acknowledges that our workers are whole people with full and sometimes complicated lives outside of the "office." And it doesn't do the company or the individual any good to make them feel they need to shut that part of themselves off when they start work each day.

Take our buddy system, for example. People going on parental leave or dealing with a serious illness can be matched with a coworker who has experienced something similar. These connections help people cope with the full range of life experiences inside and outside of work, allowing people who've gone through something challenging to share their knowledge and experience to help someone else.

Because of the independent and sometimes solitary nature of our work, cultivating connectedness is one of our primary goals in creating a great culture in our "workplace."

Collaboration, Communication, and Innovation

One of the most pervasive myths about remote work is that it stifles collaboration, communication, and innovation—that people lack those interpersonal dynamics unless they physically work together in an office.

However, our team members say they feel more connected in this virtual space than they did in jobs co-located with others. The only difference in how in-office professionals communicate versus remote professionals is the lack of in-person meetings. Most remote workers find they're able to communicate well without those, substituting office facetime with video conferencing, video calls, and occasional in-person meet-ups.

"Proactive communication" is how we approach working together: encouraging everyone to speak up, ask questions, and clarify ideas when they aren't sure about something. Also, each team sets 30-60-90-day goals, big ideas are encouraged, and processes are always being refined to foster innovation and remove roadblocks.

Because of our explicit focus on ensuring that remote work doesn't interfere with collaboration, our communication channels often work even better than some teams who all sit in the same building.

Responsibility

I saved this cornerstone of our company culture for last because it's so important. A remote work environment is built on trust—specifically, trusting everyone to act as responsible professionals capable of doing their jobs well in an independent work environment.

I've worked with some of the folks at FlexJobs for years without ever having met them in person. Our people accepted their jobs without setting foot in a traditional office or meeting face-to-face. Therefore, as a company, every level of our operation starts with a baseline of trust.

That's the key aspect of a remote company's culture. We don't have bricks and mortar. We don't have offices or water coolers, cubicles or conference rooms. Instead, the way we work together *is* our brick and mortar; it's our infrastructure.

Our company culture is the foundation of everything else we do.

UBER VS. LYFT: EXACT SAME TECH—ENTIRELY DIFFERENT CULTURES

Jeremy Swift

I can't recall ever speaking to my Uber drivers.

I pressed the button, they showed up, and off we went; transaction complete. Then one day, I switched to Lyft. Suddenly, I was chatting with my drivers. Sometimes, we talked about mundane topics, but not always. One driver told me how he stopped driving at night after an intoxicated man became verbally then physically abusive. The driver punched his attacker in self-defense, then drove the man to the hospital and called the police. Another driver told me how driving part-time allows her to go back to school and pursue a teaching degree. Another driver told me how she supplements her freelance work as a graphic designer with Lyft rides and how on several occasions those conversations with her passengers actually led to graphic design gigs.

Here's perhaps the more interesting thing I've commonly heard: although many people drive for both Uber and Lyft, they never expect to have a conversation with their Uber fares. These are virtually identical services and virtually identical platforms, yet Uber somehow fosters transactions while Lyft creates experiences.

Same basic technology—two starkly different cultures.

Same Service, Different Companies. How?

Uber has a four-year head start on Lyft—a tremendous advantage in any field but one that's especially important in tech. Uber remains the market leader, but Lyft has gained momentum, one year tripling its number of rides from the previous. There are plenty of reasons why Uber is losing ground to Lyft, but I link many of them to the company's problematic culture.

Culture, after all, is the context for our relationships, both transactional and authentic. The culture of any organization, big or small, takes its lead from the top. The good and bad of that culture permeate every level of the company, but it also extends out into the world where brand meets customer. There are plenty examples of Uber's culture problems, including reports of blatant sexual harassment, blackmailing journalists who wrote unfavorable press, and threats of physical violence against employees. But the most relevant example is Travis Kalanick himself who stepped down from his post as CEO of the company he co-founded.

The incident that sparked that was when a video surfaced of Kalanick in an ugly exchange with an Uber driver. After a public backlash, Kalanick apologized. That was the right thing to do, but Kalanick missed the larger point. An Uber driver— the only living, breathing connection between a technology platform and its customer—was telling Kalanick something about authenticity, or rather the absence of it, at Uber. What the driver was saying was that Uber needed to be a better partner.

That is where the rubber meets the road. Either you subscribe to a transactional worldview that says every engagement is an opportunity for maximizing your return on investments, or you take a more holistic view toward building authentic relationships that create value for all stakeholders over time.

The Culture *Is* the Code

Both companies allow passengers to tip, but only Lyft makes it easy for riders to do so. Sure, we're only talking about a few bucks, but the difference is huge in terms of the human experience. By making the tipping process opaque, Uber marginalizes people, and as a result, it reduces every encounter to a transaction—one which the driver can expect to be overlooked.

In contrast, Lyft makes tipping accessible and transparent, opening up the opportunity for a more authentic experience. These decisions are driven by culture, but they're enforced by computer code. While the interplay between culture and code has obvious implications for rideshare drivers and their passengers, it also permeates the rest of our society.

Have you ever unfriended someone on Facebook for political reasons? Sure, the political climate is ugly these days, but isn't unfriending someone you disagree with just as transactional as the culture at Uber? And it's not just politics. Professionally, we reduce ourselves to the narrow box of a LinkedIn profile and demand others to do the same. One of the great paradoxes of the digital revolution is that the more we connect, the more transactional we become. Our social and professional networks are huge . . . but they're also shallow. Avatars, not people, populate them. Yet all the while, we crave authenticity--not just from our leaders, but also from our friends, our spouses, and even the brands we choose to give our business to.

Tech Enables Transactions; Service Enables Connections

Sure, service can be transactional. I never had a complaint about the service rendered by my Uber drivers. But those transactions never amounted to anything more than a charge on my credit card. Whatever relationship I had with Uber wasn't authentic, and it certainly wasn't built to last.

But Lyft—that's a different story, and one every tech CEO can learn from.

3

THE SECRET WEAPON OF DISNEY, APPLE, AND THE PATRIOTS

Matt Mayberry

Have you ever stayed at a five-star hotel chain that made you feel like you were their most important guest? Have you ever visited a store or dined at a restaurant where the customer-service level far exceeded your expectations? Have you ever wondered how a sports team is in the playoffs seemingly every year?

Sure, some people are just good at what they do, and when you gather a bunch of talented people together, you're bound for success, right? Wrong. It has everything to do with a culture that is easily identifiable, attainable, and respected by everyone working within the organization. Whether your culture revolves around creating a 5-star service standard, a family environment, a winning culture, a customer-is-always-right culture, you must have one—and it must be clear—before your employees can buy into it.

Creating a distinct culture within your organization is everything. Whether in sports or business, you must set a concrete foundation and have an understanding of what your culture is—and it must be found in all that you do.

Although we often hear about the importance of culture, I still find that so many overlook how vitally important it really is. A weak culture, or one that is never firmly established, can completely diminish performance levels within an organization, even if that organization possesses the best strategies, products, and talent. On the other hand, a distinct and thriving culture can certainly make up the difference for just average strategy and talent.

Please don't get me wrong. Create the best strategies and recruit the best talent for your company. But understand that all of that is secondary to what matters most: your culture.

I have witnessed its incredible importance in my own life. During my time as an athlete, I was on teams that didn't have the most talented players in the world. We still got the job done and won games as the underdogs. That came from the result of leadership instilling a phenomenal culture from day one.

I have also been on teams with extremely talented people, but results on the field were mediocre at best. That same team lacked a definite culture. Leadership didn't set the tone of how the team should function, so it was "every man for himself." In sports, of course, the main objective is to win, but if there is no set process outside of individual talent, no set standard for all to buy into, and no leadership driving it, a star-studded roster means nothing.

In my world as a speaker now, I get the wonderful opportunity to travel and work with leaders from different industries. Prior to each speaking engagement, I sit down with the leadership of the organization to take a closer look at the culture of the organization and identify where I can add the most value. During this time, I usually find one of two things.

In some cases, I find a leader who is incredibly passionate about creating a dominant, healthy, and strong culture. These are the organizations that have great employee retention and morale.

The rest of the time, I usually find leaders who aren't as passionate about building a strong culture. They unfortunately end up falling into the trap of directing all their focus on outcomes and results. They fail to realize that a strong culture is what largely drives results. All of the championships have great strategy and talent behind them, and the sales milestones have great products and value behind them, but the culture that leadership instills and demands throughout the whole organization is what actually drives results. By focusing only on the what and how of performance—instead of the who and the why—their process ends up backfiring somewhere down the line.

I'm not telling you how to run your organization. I just want to point out the difference in results of organizations that focus on culture versus those who don't. If you take a close look at the New England Patriots, Disney, Apple, or any other organization that dominates their market or craft, you'll see they are crystal clear on the environment they want, the behavior they expect, and the experience they create—and they are single-minded in demanding those things in every aspect of their organization.

Culture is and will always be vitally important to an organization's growth, success, and longevity.

It's my hope as a leader that you make it a major priority to create a crystal-clear culture of your own.

The results will speak for themselves.

ENTREPRENEUR VOICES SPOTLIGHT: INTERVIEW WITH CAREY JUNG

President of IT Freedom

Four Times the Money, Zero Extra People

Isn't it every business owner's dream to double company revenue without hiring a single extra person?

Of course, this isn't just a dream—it's a pipe dream. Everyone knows that the way to make substantially more money is grow substantially larger. To grow substantially larger, you have to hire more people to help support that growth.

Except Carey Jung accidentally discovered that you don't.

Entrepreneur: Carey, let's start from the beginning.

Jung: I started IT Freedom here in Austin, Texas, back in 1999. From the very beginning, I wanted everyone to think like I did: as an owner. I wanted everybody to work hard, to put the greater good of the company above their own short-term gain, and to do whatever needed to be done to get the job done. I've fixed clogged toilets in the bathroom and caught rats in the break room. People who are willing to do whatever it takes like that are the kind of people I want working alongside me.

I wanted to create something that people could use for them and their families that would really give them financial security--not just some stock options, but a real ownership stake in the company--something that would grow with them.

At the time, I had no idea how to do anything like that and even I had, it wouldn't have made a difference. I had no money. I'd robbed my retirement account and put everything into the company. I spent every second and every cent on the company. But that didn't stop me from expecting an ownership mentality in my people.

Entrepreneur: How do you create a culture of ownership without the ownership?

Jung: First off, you can't expect anyone to behave like an owner if you're not willing to share in the rewards of ownership with them. We haven't always made money, and we haven't always made a lot of money. But whatever we have made, we tried to share generously in the form of profit sharing.

As we've matured over the years, learning how to manage our expenses, how to conserve cash, and consistently make money, we've continued that practice. I feel like Santa Claus at the end of every year when we hand out our bonus checks. When we did our insurance enrollment last year, our provider told us she doesn't know of another company that provides the level of benefits we do.

Share the rewards: that's our first principle.

Entrepreneur: And the second?

Jung: Sometimes as an owner, things don't always go well. Being an owner also means sharing the sacrifice.

Back in 2008, we were sailing along. Business was great. We had outgrown our offices again. We leased an entire warehouse three times the size of our then-current offices and took out a $350,000 construction loan to convert it into an office space.

We moved in May 2009, our tenth anniversary. Basically, while we were cutting the ribbon, our largest customer got bought out by a company that did all its IT in-house. We lost 40 percent of our revenue overnight. We didn't know how we were going to make it. We had a huge expense and a major loss in revenue. We restructured every note and contract that we could. Carla and I cut our salaries by 50 percent. We sold our house and moved into an apartment with our youngest daughter.

Then, the recession hit. All of our other customers started pulling back. I thought we were going to have to lay off half our staff. Even then, I wasn't sure it'd be enough. At our Friday meeting, we broke the news that we had to lay off two great people and that everyone else was getting a 10 percent pay cut immediately. They were shocked. Disappointed. Angry. We hadn't shared with them how bad things were. We realized that we hadn't treated them like the owners we said we did. After that, Carla started doing a monthly financial report at Friday lunch, which she does to this day. She goes over revenue, cost of sales, expenses, net margin, and net cash—the whole nine yards.

At first, most of us didn't understand what all those numbers meant, including me. It took Carla a lot of teaching to explain the business financial concepts to everyone.

Now, everyone in the company knows how we make money, what the bottom line is, and what their place in it is, whether it's generating top-line revenue or part of bottom-line expenses. It helps them see what's important, helps them make better decisions, and gives them confidence in the company and its leadership. For two years, we bailed and we paddled, we paddled and we bailed. It took those two years to restore everybody's salary back to what they were. It took another couple of years before Carla's and my salaries were back to what they were. But we made it.

Entrepreneur: One, share the rewards. Two, share the sacrifices. What's principle number three?

Jung: Just get better.

When I look back, I am amazed at how different of a company we are today. We have a level of operational excellent that is bar none. How did we reach that? I don't know that we necessarily work harder than anyone else or that we're smarter than anyone else. But we never settle for the status quo. We always believe that there's something that we can somehow make better. Some annoying thing we can fix, some repetitive task we can automate, or some useless task we can trash. Everyone's always looking for ways to get just a little bit better every day. Over time, that makes a huge difference.

In 2008 when things were going well, we had 18 employees. At the end of 2016, we were back up to 18 employees. But those 18 employees are generating nearly twice the revenue and four times the earnings as they were back in 2008.

Entrepreneur: Wow! Four times the money with the exact same number of employees—that's astounding!

Jung: It is amazing. That comes from having great people and all of us just making the company incrementally better over time. For example, at Friday lunch, we have a $250 drawing for people who contributed ideas that week. The more ideas you contribute, the better your chances of winning. We're not looking for brilliant ideas-- just lots of them.

It also comes from hiring the right people and promoting the right people. We have a good screening process before bringing anyone in, but most of our leaders were promoted from within the company. Our CEO, Jeff Taff, started as a network technician. Some of our best people started at the help desk.

This is the proof that we have a great culture: I've worked myself out of a job. They don't need me anymore. But more importantly for me, the culture has grown beyond me. I can go on the messaging app Slack and read those quick little messages back and forth and see the respect our people have for each other, the fun they're having, and the great work they're doing.

On our website, we keep a live ticker of customer feedback from our most recent 100 service tickets. You can rate us "excellent," "OK," or "not good." It is a rare day that we're not at 99 percent excellent. Happy employees make happy customers, and we have a 98 percent customer retention rate.

Entrepreneur: IT Freedom is now quite profitable again, you're happy, and your people are happy: what's next?

Jung: Like I said at the beginning of this interview, I've always had this idea of ownership ever since starting the company. Once we were back in the black, I started seriously thinking about it again. Around that time, one of our customers went through the process of becoming employee owned, and the more I learned about it, the more I liked it.

I've always thought it was a little disingenuous to ask employees to act like owners without making them actual owners. Profit-sharing was my solution. But with an ESOP [employee stock ownership plan], employees literally become owners. That's we decided to do.

It took a tremendous expense to set it up and it's expensive to administer the nonprofit, but I really wanted our employees to have a stake in the company they'd built. Every year now, we take a certain amount of the company's profit and sell it to our employee trust. We're now 15 percent employee-owned, and we plan to continue to increase that until the company is entirely owned by the trust.

Entrepreneur: So many entrepreneurs have seller's remorse after exiting the company they built, and then seeing it transformed by new leadership. It occurs to me that an ESOP gives you the best of both worlds. Is that your experience?

Jung: It's a great way for me to divest myself of my ownership in the company, while knowing that the culture is going to stay intact. Bringing in an outside buyer would totally disrupt our culture. They might fire half the staff and bring in completely different management. This way, with the employees gradually taking ownership of the company, it just feels right.

Today, we literally have an ownership culture.

4

YOUR CULTURE *IS* YOUR EDGE

Ben Judah

It is astounding that Blockbuster didn't start delivering DVDs by mail back in 1999. It would have effectively shut Netflix out of the market. When drones became popular, DHL and FedEx had the opportunity to begin exploring the option of drone delivery. They could have stayed ahead of the curve, but other companies are leading the charge there, too.

These recent innovations have shaken established industries across transportation, communications, retail, and logistics. The question is: why is change still coming from the outside? Why do companies and even entire industries ignore innovation, and then lose market share and industry leadership to outside challenges?

It comes down to company culture.

"It's always been done this way," is one of the most dangerous phrases to be uttered in a company, and the enforcement of that thinking is the first step on the road to ruin. The thinking that exploring new methods is dangerous is flawed for one main reason: it assumes *ceteris paribus* (from Latin; loosely, "all things remaining equal"). This can only ever occur in theory—never in reality. The world is changing faster than ever before, with cultural norms evolving to catch up with the accelerated pace of technological advancement. All things are most certainly not remaining the same, and if they do, rest assured someone somewhere has a surprise in store.

The saying goes, "Failing to prepare is preparing to fail," but whose responsibility is it to prepare? Everyone's. From the CEO to the intern, the battle cry of "none of us are as innovative as all of us" lays the foundation whereby all contributions are valid *and* welcome. Each individual within a company has his or her own area of expertise, technical or otherwise, which gives insight into new ways of innovating anything from internal processes to the overarching product or service sold. Companies that are open to hearing new ideas and are agile enough to adapt to the changing tides will stay relevant for longer and maintain market share over innovative newcomers.

WalkMe—Israel's "Most Promising Startup of 2016"—has ingrained the spirit of "there is no such thing as a bad idea." As Rafi Sweary, president of WalkMe, puts it, "One of the most important ways by which we promote innovative thinking at WalkMe is that if an idea fails, there is no negativity against the person whose idea it was. If, however, an idea is adopted successfully, the attribution and appreciation for the person who came up with the idea is seen company-wide. This created a culture in which everyone competes for innovation and efficiency in all things implemented at WalkMe."

This culture can only ever come from the top down: senior company executives must empower managers to listen and encourage the sharing of ideas from their entire team. Companies can adopt this thinking as a day-to-day occurrence or one saved for special events, creating hackathons where teams work together to intensely focus on solving complex issues or creating innovative solutions to set challenges. Hackathons started as a technique often utilized for software related businesses but now are being used as a tool to solve more issues across all different verticals.

Other companies have found ways of going one step further, in the interest of staying ahead of the curve. Google's 80/20 rule, which gave employees the opportunity to use 20 percent of their time on developing new projects, led to the creation of Gmail, Google Maps, and AdSense. Coffee behemoth Starbucks created a barista competition to keep their baristas' skills up to scratch and strive to improve with the sense of competition.

Digital content company ironSource created an internal accelerator called ironLabs which allows the 700-plus person company to behave like a small startup. Tomer bar Zeev, CEO and co-founder of ironSource, explained how useful the accelerator has been critical by saying,

> We're not only comfortable nurturing and maintaining multiple different products—that diversification is actually one of our greatest strengths. As we grew, it was imperative that we find a way to maintain that diversification, so we founded ironLabs as a space where anyone with an idea would have the resources to explore it. It worked perfectly, ensuring that we kept our

knack for agile innovation, and even birthed a new product that is now a major business element at the company.

The platform for creating innovation will always appear in different forms depending on each individual company needs and culture. It should be sacrosanct and seen as essential for the continued existence of a business.

How can you make sure you're not your market's Blockbuster but its Netflix?

FIVE COMPANIES WHO GET CULTURE RIGHT

Steffen Maier

Some companies are revered for the way they keep employees engaged and passionate about their work. Here, we share with you five of the best organizations with the most engaged staff who go the extra mile, sharing the strategies and practices that keep them at the top of the employee engagement game.

1. Full Contact

Each year, this software firm offers their employees $7,500 to take a "paid" vacation. They literally pay their people to go on holiday anywhere they like. The only rules? You actually have to go somewhere, and can't do any work or answer work related calls or messages. They stand by the idea that employees who actually go on vacation return to work with a different, fresh outlook. They are fully present and eager to get going to get back to their job.

These "paid" vacations also supposedly eliminate the issue of people thinking they're the only one who can solve a problem. Once people return from their holiday relaxed and find things running smoothly, they feel less pressure to handle everything themselves and develop a heightened sense of trust for their coworkers.

If it's not quite in your budget to give out large amounts of cash for holidays, it's always possible to let people take a couple of extra days paid leave or a long weekend once in a while. The important thing is that they can leave their work responsibilities behind and really get away. People will appreciate their efforts being recognized and welcome the chance to disconnect from their job--even for a short time.

2. Southwest Airlines

Southwest Airlines is revered for their employee engagement practices over the years. They have a team full of committed, enthusiastic people passionate about the company's vision and values. They've set the bar high as a glowing example of customer service because of their collective of happy, committed employees.

Take something as seemingly mundane as a company uniform. The company allowed employees from any department to apply to collaborate on new designs. The results reflect the personality and company culture in a way not possible had employees not been given a say. Employees were responsive to this, describing it as an "unforgettable experience."

Southwest encourages employees to do things differently, as evidenced by the viral video of one flight attendant rapping the safety information. It goes to show the kind of attitude the company has towards keeping things fun and unique by creating a great experience for customers and employees alike.

Recognizing those employees who go the extra mile is another key factor of Southwest's engagement practices. Each week, the CEO gives a "shout out," publicly praising employees who have gone above and beyond. There's also a monthly recognition in

Southwest's magazine featuring an employee who shined that month. This kind of recognition keeps employees aware that they're valued and that their commitment to the company doesn't go unnoticed.

As company founder Herb Kelleher points out, competitors can't simply adopt the levels of engagement and commitment found at Southwest—it takes a special kind of employee and company culture: "They can buy all the physical things. The things you can't buy are dedication, devotion, loyalty—the feeling that you are participating in a crusade."

3. Legal Monkeys

This legal record management company established a simpler, smaller way to show employees that their hard work is valued. Their Appreciation Board is a glass picture frame where employees can write a note and present the board to someone they want to show appreciation to. Whoever receives the board is free to keep it on display on their desk until they are ready to pass it on to someone else. Each achievement also gets posted on the company Facebook page, ensuring people outside the team see the recognition.

Ideas like this are great. They're not only simple to implement without disturbing daily workflow, but they also build a real-time feedback culture, encouraging people to give positive feedback and show appreciation for their peers and coworkers.

4. Screwfix

One way this U.K.-based hardware company keeps their employee engagement levels up is by keeping an open, honest company culture. Every two weeks, employees are given the opportunity to provide feedback without rules or guidelines to their managers. They are encouraged to give feedback on everything: how things are going, how they think things are managed, how the company interacts with customers, ideas for improvement, or anything else they want to bring to their managers' attention.

A great example of how well this initiative works: employees came up with an idea for a new customer card that speeds up the in-store process by identifying customers and allowing them to make quicker purchases. Like many other initiatives now in place, this would never have come to fruition had the employees not been asked for their input.

Having this kind of regular, 360-degree feedback in place not only means things don't get overlooked as often. It also keeps the conversation going and ensures a company culture where people feel as if they make a difference—they're more than just their role and their efforts benefit the whole company.

5. DreamWorks

Although employees at DreamWorks Animation are provided with perks such as free refreshments, paid opportunity to decorate workspaces, and company parties after big projects are completed, a practice they really appreciate is that at such parties and events, they are encouraged to share their personal work and projects with their coworkers. This opens up an appreciation of non-work related projects, boosts creativity, and makes employees feel that they are more than just the work they do for the company.

With other companies like Google also giving employees the time to work on and pitch their own projects, this is a great way to tell your employees that you not only trust them, but also that you value their input and creativity. This keeps people feeling both in control and passionate about their work.

While it may not be feasible for your company to provide huge amounts of money for "paid" holidays or assign large percentages of time to personal projects, you can take the spirit behind their practices to come up with ideas of how to implement those feelings in your own organization.

Great employee engagement is a sure-fire way to create a great company.

TO BELIEVE AND BELONG

Robert Wallace

We've all read about employees who traded jobs with great paychecks for shares in a startup. Plenty of companies have scooped up great talent for peanuts simply because they offered people a piece of the action. Many of those companies have some kind of innovative idea poised to disrupt an entire industry. The potential worth of shares in such a company is enormous.

But look deeper than just the opportunity to make a lot of money. What is it that such employees actually work for? It's not money; that's an endgame result. The reason (many, if not most) employees go to work for companies is belief: they believe in the company. They believe in the idea. They believe in its possibility.

They want to work for something they believe in.

But that emotional draw isn't just about the future—it's also about the present. They want to work with a great team. They want to enjoy their work. They want not only to believe in something, but also to belong to something.

Unfortunately, there seems to be an epidemic in the business world: founders and CEOs have the idea that they can create that kind of culture with inspirational posters, some healthy snacks, and massage chairs. That's not culture; those are nice perks. We are living in a world where people are no longer impressed by the cereal bar and spiral slide to the breakroom. Employees of today want to be inspired. They need to trust the brand they are handing their talent, time, and effort to. If you want to build an organization that draws, keeps, and engages the best and brightest, you have to start with your core values.

Core Values Tell Stories (And Vice Versa)

Phrases like "integrity," "people first," and "passion" are used by everyone (or at least should be). These are the right ideas. However, the words themselves won't set you apart. Skim any of the hiring profiles on CareerBuilder or Monster.com, and you'll see hundreds of job listings using these buzz words. But there's no brand, values, or story behind them. They just know what they're supposed to say.

Core values tell stories. By definition, core values are the guiding principles that dictate behavior and action. Values are things that you can tell specific stories about: stories of when a colleague did something amazing for a customer or a teammate. If you can't tell a story about something you've listed, it's not a real value.

You Already Have Core Values, But . . .

If you are an established company, you have an advantage. Sure, your framed core values plaque is probably due for a good dusting, but as a functioning company with employees and customers, you already have stories to draw from.

The first step is dusting off the plaque and really evaluating what you've narrowed your values down to. Do they speak to the services your company provides? Do they evoke an emotion that is specific to your company and what you do on a daily basis? There are plenty of examples to draw from. The biggest thing you can do is to get your team involved. By asking your employees or managers what they think the core values really are, you'll get priceless insight and real life examples.

Once you've evaluated and/or chosen your values, imagine yourself in an interview. Your core values should help you make decisions on hiring and firing. Many of today's most admired companies hire for culture first and skill second. If a potential employee were to ask you what one of the company's values meant, could you draw from a real life experience from you or your team?

Be unique, and let your core values tell your story.

It's Too Early to Define Your Values ... Right?

As a younger company, you may only have a co-founder and a dream. This means you have the perfect opportunity to create an outline for the stories you want to tell. By creating meaningful core values, new employees will be able to make better decisions if they know to align their daily activities with the core values.

If communicated properly, your team will know how to respond to tough customers, how to treat fellow teammates, and even start a path to career growth—all based on the foundation that you've built for them. Regardless of the size of the company, as a leader, be sure to commend people publicly when they demonstrate a value. Just as importantly, tell them when they haven't (but perhaps not publicly).

Core values carry a lot of weight but, unfortunately, often go overlooked after the first 30 days of employment. When embraced properly, core values become part of your day-to-day activities within your company's walls and beyond. They form a compass for performance and the stories you tell when asked about your business. Make them matter.

Everyone wants to work for a company they believe in.

Give them something worth believing in.

ENTREPRENEUR VOICES SPOTLIGHT: INTERVIEW WITH MICHAEL BUSH

CEO of Great Place to Work

Better Culture = Better Business

Michael Bush is the CEO of a great place to work.

Literally.

Each year, *Fortune* magazine partners with the research company Great Place to Work to create *Fortune*'s "100 Best Companies to Work For" list. Why? Because Great Place to Work has been collecting data and refining its analyses for over 20 years.

In those two decades, Great Place to Work has surveyed over 100 million employees on everything from career opportunities to discrimination to peer respect. If anyone knows what it takes to create a great company culture, these people do.

Entrepreneur: Michael, what does it take to create a great place to work?

Bush: For entrepreneurs, it really starts with the first hire an entrepreneur makes. You go from being an individual to a two-person organization. That's when the values start to get created.

Entrepreneur: That's a great point. When we say "culture," we often think of a group of employees, but you're saying it's important to be aware of culture even when it's just the entrepreneur and someone answering the phone, right?

Bush: That's right. An entrepreneur already has a set of things that they believe in. There are certain things they are willing to do to grow their business and certain things they're not willing to do. All of those things come from a certain set of beliefs or values that they have. Those form the initial values of the company.

So many entrepreneurs hire someone or find a partner and bring them on board thinking they're magical—the yin to their yang. More often than not, those partnerships fall apart or those first hires quit or get fired. When you talk to these entrepreneurs and examine their experience from the perspective of values, you often see the partnership or employment fell apart because of a difference in values.

Entrepreneur: It sounds like you would argue that an entrepreneur knowing their values and looking for people who fit in with those—i.e., someone who is culturally aligned—is critical even before the very first person they bring on board.

Bush: Successful entrepreneurs are the ones who find the people who share their values and work with them to grow the company. They may not have defined their values at that point, but they innately know that this person does business the way they like to do business.

But if you want a high performance culture, you have to know what your values are. You have to write them down and share them with people. When you hire, it's as important to hire based on those values as it is to hire for people's skills and competence.

Entrepreneur: Hiring the right people is something that crops up again and again in discussions on culture. Obviously, Great Place to Work has the numbers to underscore the importance of that. But what about once you hire the right person? Does culture take care of itself?

Bush: Once you hire them, you have to build on those values. We've identified the three factors every great place to work shares: respect, credibility, and fairness.

People need to feel that they're being respected by their coworkers and their managers. They need to believe that people are telling the truth and being transparent. They need to know that there are no favorites. When those things are true, people bring all of themselves to work. They bring their enthusiasm, their ideas, and their passion. That's when you get innovation: when people can bring all that they are to work.

We have the evidence that shows that when people are in a high trust environment—that is, when there is respect, credibility, and fairness—there is a demonstrable difference in performance. Companies with a high sense of trust outperform their peers in virtually every hard metric you analyze.

However, our research shows us that in organizations, you often have pockets of people who feel that they are not respected like everyone else. They don't feel that company leadership is telling them the truth. They do feel that some people are treated better than others. They don't feel that they're accepted in the workplace. That company may be a great place to work for some people, but not for all people. For whatever reason, the values of the company aren't being experienced by these particular people.

That's why it's so important that leaders continually assess their culture. They need to ensure that everyone is experiencing a high-trust environment. Otherwise, they will never benefit from all that that employee has to offer.

Entrepreneur: What I love about your evidence is that you can quantify the idea that superior culture leads to superior profit—that doing the right thing for your people aligns with doing well financially. Culture is not a philanthropic exercise but a strategic advantage.

Bush: That's right.

A few research and academic institutions have analyzed all the companies on the S&P 500 over the last 20 years. The companies on our list of the best places to work outperformed the S&P by a factor of three-to-one.

Entrepreneur: Wow! Three-to-one! That number tells the tale, doesn't it?

Bush: There was a *Fortune* article in March of 2017 where the founder of the mutual fund Parnassus Endeavor, Jerry Dodson, talks about the millions of dollars his fund has made investing in the companies on our "100 Best Places to Work For" list with Fortune.

Entrepreneur: What's your advice to entrepreneurs defining the values for their companies?

Bush: One of the things we see is when a business owner states that the company values are one thing, but when you talk to their employees, you find that the leaders don't follow those values. The entrepreneur has defined aspirational values—something that they would like to be true or that sound good—but those stated values don't reflect the entrepreneur's real values.

At that point, you have a credibility issue. What you say and what you do are two different things. Without credibility, you don't have a high-trust environment. Without that, you won't have employees who bring all of themselves to work.

Take time to discover your values. Think about what's important to you. Look at what other people are doing and how strongly you agree or disagree with it. Talk to your friends and family about what they see as important to you. Show them the values you've written and ask them if that's been their experience with you.

Many entrepreneurs will meet someone and feel like they have a real connection with them. They might skip over sharing their values with that person because they feel that they know them so well. Maybe it's even a long-time friend or family member. In those cases, there's actually an even bigger need to write those values down. Personal relationships can sometimes blind you to the differences you have.

Be careful when you're defining your values that you're not trying to do a beautiful job to shape someone else's image of you: "Look at my values! Don't they look good? This means I'm a good person."

Really, you want some values that are controversial. For the people who have a problem with those values, it will push them away; you can discover early on that they're not a good fit for your company. But for the people who do share those values, it will make them want to be part of your company even more.

Entrepreneur: Michael, let's fast forward a few years. Say an entrepreneur wasn't intentional about their culture and things have gotten away from them. How do you fix a dysfunctional culture?

Bush: It happens quite frequently. Entrepreneurs are busy getting started, getting their cash flow worked out, hiring people, and securing office space. The idea of defining company culture may not even be on their list of the million things they have to do. So culture gets put to the side where it sits until it becomes a major issue that has to be addressed. Then, it becomes something that has to be "fixed."

First, I'd advise the entrepreneur to make sure they were looking at this topic through the right lens: culture isn't a problem that needs to be fixed but an opportunity they're not taking advantage of. Without a high-trust culture, they're wasting an enormous amount of talent, innovation, productivity, and leadership. They need to know how things stand by surveying their employees. They need the facts of what their people's experiences at work are.

Once they know where they are, then they have to compare the entrepreneur's honest values with the reality of their company. What aspects are out of alignment? Why don't they have an environment of respect, credibility, and fairness?

What we often find are those pockets of unfairness where there's one culture for the sales team but another culture for the back office or one culture for managers and another culture for the line-workers. That limits your growth and potential. When we work with companies to develop an action plan on these issues, I can tell you one of the recommendations that always make it into the top three: listening. Employees at all levels want to know that they have a voice that is heard.

That's how you make a great place to work for all.

PART I
CLARITY—REFLECTIONS

The results speak for themselves . . . but we're going to talk about them anyway.

From Carey Jung's fourfold increase in earnings with the same number of employees to the companies on the Great Place to Work list outperforming the S&P 500 by three-to-one—you just can't argue with these kinds of results. You can't afford *not* to take company culture seriously.

As the piece on Uber vs. Lyft demonstrated, culture is your competitive advantage. As the barriers to entry continue to fall in virtually every industry, as technology levels the playing field, as geography is less and less of any kind of differentiator, and as global talent can virtually ignore borders—that is, *ceteris paribus*, as one of our authors said—culture becomes the only competitive advantage left.

As the CEO of Great Place to Work said of entrepreneurs: you need to clarify what's important to you now and make sure that your company embodies those values even when it's just you and someone answering the phone. That way, if and when your team grows to 6 or 60 or 600, your vision has already been embedded in the foundation of your organization.

Robert Wallace's article speaks to a profound idea: When people leave a job to go work for a new business, they do so because they believe in the company. Yes, it may be that they believe in its growth potential and trade salary for stock, but even in those instances, it's still because they believe in the company itself. Let that sink in for a moment: people are willing to risk it all for a company they believe in.

What's more, the range of companies held up as examples in this section span from the 18 people at IT Freedom to the 188,000 people at Publix (from the Great Place to Work list of the 100 best). Ergo, pursuing an awesome culture isn't limited by size. Nor is it limited by industry, as those two companies also show; one provides IT services while the other is a grocery store. Not even geography is apparently a factor, as FlexJobs shows. In short, there's no excuse. You can create a great culture regardless of your company.

So let's talk about how to effectively lead it.

LEADING

T he first section of this book spoke mostly about companies. This second section speaks mostly about you, the company's leader.

Entrepreneurs don't often have an issue with assuming responsibility and spearheading new ideas. That's what makes them entrepreneurial to begin with. But when it comes to company culture, it's not always easy for the founder to be brutally honest with themselves—to see that whatever happens in a company is most often a reflection of themselves, much like looking into a mirror. But if you want to create the kind of culture you've envisioned, the mirror is exactly where these contributors say you have to begin.

When a company grows to mammoth proportions, culture is diffused more. It's more difficult to effect change at that size (but not impossible). But your company is most likely still at the size where your own behavior carries substantial impact. Indeed, that flexibility and agility is usually one of the primary advantages smaller companies have over their market-dominating peers.

That means that the advice you're about to read about leading a great company culture—much of it virtually free to implement—is advice that you can use and see results from immediately.

Isn't that the exciting part about being an entrepreneur? That you can have an idea in the morning and put it into action by that afternoon? That there are worlds of possibilities? That the future is not some place you're journeying to, but a reality that you shape with every decision?

The writers you're about to read believe that, too.

7

THE LEADER SETS THE CULTURE

Brian Patrick Eha

You are leading the culture of your company workplace. The only question is: are you doing it intentionally, or are you doing it unconsciously? Let's look at four different organizations and how the leaders at each one got explicit about shaping their company culture.

Leading a Culture of Teamwork

In 2012, chef Niki Nakayama was living her dream, preparing traditional Japanese *kaiseki* feasts at her Los Angeles restaurant, n/naka. Then, her sous chef quit without notice. "I had been accustomed to splitting tasks with him," she says, but everything fell on her shoulders. She dove in, preparing exquisite, labor-intensive meals of 9 or 13 courses—but with less leadership available, her minimal staff suffered.

What was going on?

The problem may have been culture. In traditional Japanese kitchens—not unlike some traditional American offices—subordinates are expected to watch and learn, rarely ask questions, and never debate the head chef's ideas. "I am not a great teacher," Nakayama admits. That's why the loss of her sous chef was so acute: The staff had lost a certain kind of leader, someone who could "speak Niki," bringing order to her creative chaos and translating her instructions for everyone else. Nakayama couldn't fill the hole herself.

She came to a realization: Everyone should be aware of their weaknesses and overcome them as a team. Nakayama fixed her own problem by hiring Carole Iida, a fellow chef. Where Nakayama was messy and spontaneous, working off the top of her head, Iida was organized and reliable, and could guide the staff. "She brought in her organizational abilities, and we were able to put everything together for other people to understand," Nakayama says.

As a result, the 2016 Zagat guide has awarded n/naka the top spot for food among L.A. restaurants, a dramatic rise from the year before. Now, Nakayama encourages all her workers to focus on their strengths—"to pull out that best part of ourselves and just contribute that all the time without spending too much time trying to fix the weaknesses that we have," she says. "It's far more productive in a team environment. It's knowing and respecting each other's strengths and weaknesses that makes a great team."

Leading a Culture of Rigor

The well-regarded nonprofit research center Santa Fe Institute (SFI) sets a high bar for scientific inquiry. More than 250 researchers affiliated with SFI are investigating the fundamentals behind the world's biggest problems, from plagues to global economics. Its president and William H. Miller Professor of Complex Systems, accomplished scientist David Krakauer, knows one thing for sure: When working with all these great minds, he cannot always be the smartest one in the room. He sometimes thinks of himself "as a colonel leading an army of generals."

So, how does he lead them? "The authority of my position is not worth shit," he says. "When I'm talking to someone who is more accomplished than I am, my opinion is not the most compelling argument. The most compelling argument is rigor. You have to speak the language of rigor."

To "Speak the language of rigor" means to support every idea with observation, evidence, and analysis—and maybe even conducting experiments to determine the best course of action. It means trusting a clear, quantitative approach that everyone can understand, and it means not using language that's limiting.

Here's a phrase Krakauer hates: "That's not how we do things around here." No. He is adamant on this point: anyone caught uttering that phrase, he says, "should be put down."

Like scientists, business leaders should wield evidence as a tool of persuasion, Krakauer believes. He quotes physicist Richard Feynman, "Science is the belief in the ignorance of experts." It's a hard lesson to learn, but a necessary one: Your gut instinct is not sufficient. If you want to persuade top talent to follow your lead, you'd better be able to back up your arguments with more than your job title.

Leading a Culture of Inquiry

The tech startup Contently helps Fortune 500 companies and other brands engage in content marketing. Founded by three guys in New York in 2010, it has since grown to a staff of about 100. Along the way, cofounder and chief creative officer Shane Snow feared a disturbing change: The energy driving that growth—that scrappy, do-anything attitude—could easily diminish or even disappear. Employees might become timid in large groups, afraid of earning the ire of the majority.

"Most people and most companies reach a plateau at a certain point, and at many points," says Snow. "It's crazy how quickly even a disruptive, rebellious startup can get to the point where they say, 'That's not the way things are done here.'"

There's that phrase again.

Contently took steps to make sure that culture didn't take root. For one, Snow limits meetings that involve problem solving—that is, a situation where employees really need to speak up—to three or four people. Employees are game, Snow says: They do want to keep things fresh. A leader's role is to create the right opportunities. He challenges Contently's big team to feel scrappy by doing things like asking for ten X ideas—say, "How can we improve customer happiness by ten times?"

Time for another forbidden phrase: "Don't bring me problems; bring me solutions." Leaders use that phrase because they think it inspires employees to take initiative, says Adam Grant, a professor at the University of Pennsylvania's Wharton School and author of *Originals: How Non-Conformists Move the World* (Viking, 2016). Instead, it teaches employees not to speak up about a need unless they have a proposal for fixing it.

"When you ask for solutions, you create a culture of advocacy rather than a culture of inquiry," Grant says. "Most creativity--most innovation--happens when somebody points out a problem that's not yet been solved."

Snow wants to hear it all. He and his cofounders set aside a few free hours every week so any employee who wants to chat can do so. It's an invitation to hear about those problems that are in search of solutions. "When someone brings in a perspective that hasn't been heard yet," Grant says, "it often forces you to reconsider your decision criteria, to bring in new information—and that ultimately is good for your process."

Leading a Culture of Accountability

Bridgewater Associates is the world's largest hedge fund, managing over $150 billion in assets for sovereign wealth funds, corporate and public pensions, foundations, and university endowments. Its founder, Ray Dalio, is widely seen as a financial genius. Yet after a meeting with a potential client one day, an employee several levels down on the org chart fired off a blistering email to Dalio. He accused the boss of being unprepared and disorganized, going so far as to give him a D-mins grade for his behavior!

"I don't know many organizations where you can send an email like that to the billionaire founder and keep your job," says Grant in *Originals*. But instead of lashing out, Grant says Dalio asked others who had participated in the meeting to assess his performance. The email exchange was then forwarded to the entire staff, effectively turning Dalio's misstep into a case study.

This is how Bridgewater's culture works, according to Grant--everyone is accountable to everyone. The staff is expected to routinely rate coworkers on a range of 77 qualities, including some—like the willingness to touch a nerve—that might not be prized at other companies. The firm's 1,500 employees can even assess their bosses; the more incisive the critique, the better. All this data, including the name of each person who left feedback, is available to any employee.

It's extreme. It wouldn't work for most companies. Thirty-five percent of new hires don't make it past 18 months. But consider what Bridgewater is going for: It wants employees to feel that hard work is recognized, and that the company values transparency. Find ways to bring those traits into your workplace—because when an employee feels comfortable enough to challenge you, and you're able to turn that into a lesson in leadership, then you've created a culture in which everyone can do their best work.

Dalio's example is perhaps the most illustrative of all the examples here. It shows just how far a CEO has to go in leading company culture. What happens at Bridgewater is what happens everywhere—culture starts at the top.

THE UNICORN WITH A "NO SHOES" OFFICE

Rose Leadem

Imagine walking into an office for a professional meeting and upon opening the door you're welcomed by a crowd of busy, *shoeless* workers. What's more, before you go any further, you too have to take off your shoes.

Welcome to Gusto.

Gusto is an online payroll, benefits, and HR service that seeks to reimagine and simplify human resource practices for businesses across America.

One of the brains behind Gusto and this shoe-less office is its CEO and co-founder, Joshua Reeves.

Why the "no shoes" policy? Reeves was raised in a no-shoes household. When he and his co-founders began working on Gusto in an upstairs bedroom of a Palo Alto house, they continued the tradition. Though the company began to grow, the tradition remained.

Even before Gusto, Reeves was no stranger to Silicon Valley. Prior to the HR company, Reeves was the CEO and co-founder of startup Unwrap. Facing one of his toughest business decisions ever, Reeves and the team decided to sell Unwrap to Context Optional in 2010. It didn't take long before Reeves was wrapped up in his newest and greatest venture. In 2011, Reeves and his co-founders Edward Kim and Tomer London launched Gusto.

Six years and 450 employees later, Gusto has become a leading all-in-one HR platform supporting modern companies across the U.S. Valued at $1.1 billion, the company serves more than 40,000 customers with offices in San Francisco and Denver.

With experience running two successful companies in the competitive Bay Area, it's no doubt that Reeves knows a thing or two about being an effective leader. Here's Reeves' take on leading workplace culture.

What's culture?

There's no right or wrong culture—there are many ways to build a company and many ways to have a culture. I think what's most important is leaders in a company being opinionated and being authentic. It should be a byproduct of what feels natural.

Culture is simply your values and your traditions. Traditions are things that develop organically, and values are things that are very core. It's spending the time to understand what that core value system is and in the way it's maintained, and that should really drive hiring.

We have three pillars to hiring, and it's all about alignment—values alignment, motivations alignment and skill set alignment. For values and motivation, every company is different, and you have to find out what you stand for. Motivation is hugely important, because motivation proves if someone really cares about the problem we're fixing and if they're really going to be proud and excited.

In some ways, Gusto every six to 12 months is almost a whole new company because there are a bunch of new people. So a lot of the puzzles that I think about are around scaling: What's right for a 450-person company vs. a 50-person company? At 50, I was the one that could talk to everyone: I made every offer; I onboarded each person. That doesn't scale.

It forces you to revisit the question of what is right for this next phase of Gusto, not just what's worked really well in the past. And that matters in hiring, too. Who is the right person for this role, for this next phase of Gusto?

I do welcome workshops every two weeks with every person joining Gusto. They're mostly a discussion around our values, our mission, and our market. I tell everyone this is how I connect to these values and this is why I care about the problem we're trying to fix for small businesses. And you're here because I know you also care about it because that's why you joined. This is my company, this is your company, we're all equity holders—this is our business.

At every welcome workshop, I play a video clip from Steve Jobs. It's a 1995 video clip where he talks about how the world around us was created by people that are no smarter than us and how we can change this world, we can improve it, and we can make our mark upon it. If you poke life, it will poke back.

What's your role in leading culture?

I think the first one is introspection—understanding yourself, understanding your motivations and your values, as well as having a sense of what you stand for and what drives you.

Second, I think it's really important to realize that my role is to be of service, to be a steward, to go enable others to do great work. In our org charts, I'm at the bottom—I'm here to enable and empower others.

And then the third is being ok not knowing something and being ok being wrong at times. I would call this "growth mindset"—constantly wanting feedback and realizing that everything we do can get better. There's no top of the mountain. It's just a continual climb to improve.

My leadership style is to make sure that everyone at Gusto understands what our due north is—our purpose, our mission—and have that be baked into our hiring. But from there, I'm a steward. I'm a guide to help us navigate that journey.

What habits help you lead?

Introspection. Every day, I either try to garden or go on a run. It's very therapeutic and invaluable to realize, especially in nature, all of the things that are much bigger and broader than us. Exercise is great because it's a repetitive action; you can have the mind wander. Daydreaming is really valuable. It's not a time of being in control to look at an email or to respond to a message or to speak about a specific topic. I try not to have anything smartphone related 30 minutes after waking up and 30 minutes before bed.

More professionally, at least monthly, I go through how I spend my time and how it was aligned with how I intended to spend my time.

How do you individually reinforce culture?

I think even prior to that is making sure that there's an alignment around what the goal is and what success is. So, the heart of that conversation is the one-on-one that happens between the individual and their manager. At Gusto, you talk to your manager, you share with them what goals you have, they share with you the goals the company has, you find alignment, and you get feedback. And when something is successful, there should be really strong validation of that.

How do you corporately reinforce culture?

A number of ways.

When I join meetings, I go in very deliberately making sure people understand whether I'm the decision-maker or if I'm there to give input. It's important to clarify that because people tend to be biased in not wanting to disagree with a leader. I think it's really important if the leader is not the decider or just is giving an opinion, it could definitely be wrong. We're all just people. I'm not going to have all the ideas—I want people to agree or disagree and push back often.

Early on, we would do something called a "work-cation," which was the whole company spending a week in an Airbnb and basically doing a hackathon. We would choose projects on the first day, organize into teams, and then do presentations on Friday of what we worked on. We would also go hiking and do outdoor activities.

With the larger company now, we do something we call "Gustoway." It's something we do annually, and it evolves every year. Last year we did it at a Boy Scout camp and it was mostly a set of workshops, plus just relaxing, having a campfire, and enjoying being in nature.

I think these things should feel really organic. It should feel like a community—these are people that care about each other and we want that to feel natural and to create these different programs to augment that.

Where do most Leaders go wrong on culture?

I think a very clear pitfall is thinking that the way others do something is the way you should do it. It's an interesting dynamic. As an individual, what makes someone most successful is doing it their own way. In school, if you're going to study for an exam, it's all on you. Once you understand your best way to study, you can be successful—but there are many ways to study.

You need to lead your culture according to what's important to you.

EXPAND WITHOUT KILLING CULTURE

Tony Delmercado

You've done the cost/benefit analysis, scoped out your next city location, acquired the capital, and jumped in. Congratulations: you're ready to expand!

Expansion is exciting and overwhelming—much the way the early days were for you when you first dealt with a lot of moving pieces. But this time, to ensure success now, you have to figure out how to keep your culture strong and intact *before* you launch your new location.

Take Philz Coffee, for example. Even though the San Francisco-based company has over 40 stores, each one feels like a small-town coffee shop. That's the down-home vibe that CEO Jacob Jaber wants to preserve. Philz' expansion's big challenge is to maintain that atmosphere for every location.

Dreaming of similar growth? If you're looking to expand to more cities, it's possible to proactively prepare your new employees to become part of your awesome company culture.

Your First Key Hire

Before you open for business in another city, your most important hire is the new site's leader. Make sure you have the time and resources to vet all candidates before you make a decision. That means flying them out for extensive interviews and meeting them in their cities to see them in action on their home turf.

If you don't take these crucial precautions, you could end up with a manager who is a poor cultural fit. Leaders at new locations must be strong proponents of your company culture or they won't be on the same page with headquarters. That kind of misalignment won't bode well for the future success of a new site. When leaders don't embody core values, you'd better believe no one else in that office will either.

In our own company, we learned this the hard way after expanding into what we'll call City A— we're using the pseudonym to protect the identities of those involved. While we really liked the guy we chose to manage our new site, he wasn't our typical hire. At the time, we thought it would be beneficial to get some fresh perspectives and ideas, and we spent barely any time with him before setting him loose.

In City B, however, things were different. We flew the new manager to our home office for a full week, visited with him regularly, and met him at conferences in other cities. In other words, we spent a great deal of time vetting him, and he's been a great asset to our company as a result.

Having invested the time and energy to hire someone we knew was aligned with our culture; we're seeing much more success in City B than in City A.

The extra effort was well worth it.

Show Off—Early and Often

When you expand to a new site, you want people (including prospective employees) to know who you are and understand that you have clout. New research from Deloitte suggests that bad employer reputation is one of the top potential threats to employee engagement. On the flip side, a good reputation is a huge factor in attracting and retaining talent.

To prime the market for us and establish the same reputation we enjoy in our home city, we've hosted public events in new cities before launching there. We've considered these to be cultural expressions with which we can show locals and potential employees how our company operates and what we value.

So, do the same. Take that kind of strategy to whatever corner of the market you're trying to conquer. Pump up the leader of your new office in front of the community, and when you finally do put roots down, you'll find that people will be clambering to work there.

Show Up—Early and Often

A satellite office is essentially an island. Before long, employees may begin to feel disengaged from the company as a whole. To preempt this happening, help new folks understand and embrace your culture up-front. Conduct a group activity that aligns with one of your core company values.

Are many of your new site's employees recent college graduates? According to research from Cone Communications, 83 percent of participating Millennials said they were more loyal to companies committed to their communities. So, if environmental sustainability is important to you, for instance, you might let your new employees experience your culture firsthand through a volunteer effort to clean up a beloved but polluted river.

This kind of collaboration not only creates camaraderie among different offices, but it also helps employees understand how your culture guides their behavior at work. An added bonus is that it might get your group showcased in the local news. (Hello! Free PR!)

Communicating your company culture to new staff members at satellite locations, then, is a critical first step on the road to successful expansion. Your thriving culture is a competitive advantage, and taking the time to plan and replicate it across all your sites is the key to a healthy bottom line and continued growth.

Shout Out—Early and Often

Digital communication platforms can be amazing to help you build bridges across offices, states, and even countries. Luckily, the tools we use—the 7Geese digital recognition and engagement platform and the project management tool Wrike—have helped us foster a strong sense of cohesion among our distributed team members.

Here's the thing. Even if you're sitting 20 feet away from someone, you might not necessarily give her a high-five after she's done a killer job on something. We suggest that everybody recognize five other people each quarter as well as post something positive about every client every week within our digital systems. This gets people charged up and helps everyone feel more connected.

Before you expand, make a plan to replicate any digital communication systems your home office uses in satellite offices. Recognizing one another's accomplishments publicly, and celebrating wins together, goes a long way toward unifying culture across distant sites.

STOP LOSING GOOD PEOPLE BECAUSE OF BAD CULTURE

Pratik Dholakiya

A report by Dale Carnegie Training found that a collective $11 billion is lost each year in the process of re-hiring, re-training, and re-development. The end goal for shaping culture in the workplace should be a professional environment where employees *want* to stick around for the long haul.

How?

1. Lead by Example

Throughout history, one of the most commonly observed characteristics in effective leaders has been their ability to work on the front lines with their subordinates. Theodore Roosevelt's style was a prime example of this idea.

You can demand respect all you want. But to actually earn it, you need to project a mentality conveying the message that no task is beneath you and that you wouldn't make anyone do something you wouldn't do yourself.

In addition to exhibiting the fearless leader mindset so many founders aspire to, there is an array of small habits you should get into. For example, make it a point to be the first one to arrive at work. If you consistently show up late, you are basically condoning others to do the same.

In short, your company culture is an extension of your own ethics and professional image. You are a living, breathing model for what your brand should exemplify.

2. Make Smart Hires

You can do only so much to shape a professional culture on your own. The people you choose to surround yourself with will play a huge role in how the company operates. For this reason, be picky about whom you bring on board.

During the interview stage, your goal should be to gauge the candidate's long-term vision and professional mentality. Truth be told, coming up with answers to those classic interview questions isn't terribly difficult. This is why it can be beneficial for you to ask more off-beat questions where the answers will yield information about who the candidate is as a real person.

Zappos prides itself on hiring talent aligned with its cultural expectations. The company knows that when candidates fit in with its workplace environment, operations will run more smoothly in all aspects.

Ask candidates about their hobbies outside of work. If they have any that provide a stream of income, this shows they are valuable on multiple levels and have a "go-getter" mindset.

Another good topic is the candidate's life as a student. As many people know, college is an incredibly chaotic time when young developing professionals must perform in the classroom, make money, and maintain a social life. Ask about what this person did to prioritize and execute tasks during college. Did they pay attention to their health? What were some of the most valuable lessons this person walked away with?

The people you hire should embody what you want the culture to be. Learning how they manage their day-to-day life is a building block for a high-performing operation.

3. Embrace Feedback

It's no secret that the top-down management style doesn't resonate well in today's workplace. As an entrepreneur, you have most likely grown used to your own way of doing things. However, when you start involving more people, you must be open-minded to what they have to say. Just because it's your business doesn't make other ideas irrelevant.

Soliciting regular feedback from employees is critical to advance a culture. Great leaders listen and facilitate. Try introducing feedback forms or set aside an hour every month to discuss how things are going. The objective should be to identify bottlenecks and find the best ways to solve issues.

A company culture is not something that is set in stone. It's a constantly developing entity which can change by the day. This is why you must emphasize the importance of checking in and encourage people to be honest about the company's direction.

4. Celebrate Victories

Everyone likes to feel appreciated. As a leader, when you tie individual accomplishments to the big picture, employees gain a sense of purpose and gratification that their efforts are paying off.

If the company had a great quarter, month, or even week, show your appreciation. Buy everyone lunch on Friday, sponsor a company happy hour, or host a party. By constantly giving employees something to look forward to, you'll be motivating people to do their best work. A company culture isn't grown just inside the office during business hours. Hosting events in celebration of good performance is one of the best ways to keep morale up.

Think of your company culture as the foundation of a house. If it's poorly designed and executed, one bad storm could cause the entire building to crumble. But remember, like Rome, a great culture isn't built in a day.

WHICH CAME FIRST: THE CULTURE OR THE GROWTH?

Tony Delmercado

Startups that grow into big corporations share many of the same characteristics: innovation, resilience, agility, and passion. However, startups can't successfully build on these crucial traits without the foundation of a strong company culture. In essence, each of these qualities is a product of culture.

Where Does Culture Come From?

If culture makes the business, you'd think most people would agree on what drives it. But a 2016 survey from the Workforce Institute at Kronos tells a different tale: A third of human resources professionals claim to take the lead on culture, while 26 percent of managers believe the executive team defines it.

Throw employees into the mix, and opinions diverge further. One-third of them feel they drive culture, and another 28 percent maintain that *no one* is accountable for creating or destroying it.

Disagreement about who drives, creates, or is capable of damaging culture indicates that an organization's culture isn't aligned with its business objectives. If those are two different talking points, it's hard to unite everyone through culture.

Consider this: assume you've just hired a bunch of employees. Afterward, you read about a cool office that meets regularly for happy hours. Trying to adopt this strategy out of nowhere will feel backward. If happy hours weren't mentioned at onboarding, your team won't see them as an authentic expression of your culture. When leaders try to retrofit something on top of an existing framework, it's often met with resentment. Culture is fundamental throughout the process; you can't focus on it after the fact.

For instance, take the acquisition of Virgin America by Alaska Air. Both organizations come to the table with very different cultures. The challenge will be blending them together into a new entity that represents what it plans to become in the future.

How do you start everyone at your company on the same culture page?

Define Yourself as an Individual

An entrepreneur's company culture mirrors who they are on a personal level. Our company culture has three main components: get sh*t done, learn quickly, and be cool (in other words, "don't be a jerk"). These maxims flow directly from the traits that helped my partner and me find success in our own lives.

I've tried before to instill a culture that wasn't true to me, but I felt like I was faking it. Now, I'm the same guy at work as I am in the rest of my life. To get to the heart of your culture, go beyond the surface and ask yourself hard questions about who you are as a person: are you strong, weak, confident, or effective? Find your core values and beliefs, and align them with your business objectives to create a thriving culture.

Start with Your Very First Hire

Culture should be the first thing a new hire observes. Our culture statement can be seen in every position we advertise, offer letter, and employee handbook. Everywhere new hires look, they see our three core values.

Zappos also takes orientation very seriously, devoting four weeks to the process. From day one, new hires hear about its "holocratic" approach to running the business. There are no real job titles, no managers, and no hierarchy. If that approach doesn't suit a new employee, the company even offers a buyout of one month's salary.

Define culture when you have fewer employees, as it's easier for one person to change the mood in a room of four than it is in a crowd of 100. The members of that small team will eventually serve as cultural ambassadors for new hires. As the company grows, the core values from your early days will flourish.

Align Business Decisions with Culture

For more than 80 percent of employers, cultural fit is a top priority in hiring decisions—including the hiring and firing of clients. Everyone you work with and every decision you make should align with your culture. If they don't, friction, conflict, and confusion are bound to arise. We've certainly let go of clients who didn't exemplify our core value regarding partnerships (be cool).

For example, we once developed a game plan for two clients that was on-point with what they wanted from the start. But, for whatever reason, they were consistently disrespectful, rude, and insulting— despite positive results. So, we fired them. Exposing employees to that sort of negativity isn't good for morale.

Yammer, a social network owned by Microsoft, takes a similarly forthright approach to evaluating new hires. It eliminated nearly 30 percent of its engineers within the first four years because they lacked the skills needed to drive success, dragging other employees down with them.

Make Corrections Public

People might discuss culture in closed-door meetings at other companies, but we address issues that support and bolster or go against our culture publicly. We do the same when correcting them.

Recently, someone at the company said I was being negative every morning in stand-up, so I made a note to myself that said, "Praise in public; criticize individually in private." If I start seeing a theme, however, I'll take it public.

As former L.A. Lakers coach Phil Jackson said, "I've found that anger is the enemy of instruction." So I'm not going to berate people publicly for making mistakes they probably already feel bad about.

There Is No Magic Wand

You can't wave a magic wand and expect people to accept a culture without some sort of precedence and grounding. You set the example for your first hires, they set the example for the second round, and so on.

The truth is that you need to set the example—and set it early—for every employee at your company. Align your culture with your core beliefs and your business objectives, and don't be afraid to correct missteps. Regardless of what people think about who sets the culture in other companies, it's up to you to set the tone for yours.

12

SIMPLIFY THE WORKPLACE

Anka Wittenberg

Simplification is a major initiative for many organizations, including SAP. By reducing complexity and striving for simplicity, we know that companies can develop new opportunities for competitive advantage. In contrast, firms that cling to complex processes, structures, and tools hold themselves back. In a recent Knowledge@ Wharton study, 74 percent of respondents said that complexity hurts their ability to meet goals.

The cost of complexity is significant. Authors Simon Collinson and Melvin Jay characterize complexity as one of the biggest challenges facing modern business. They write that complexity "is slowing companies down, costing them on average 10 percent of their profits and harming employee morale."

Complexity also has a negative impact on employees. Studies have shown that trust, diversity, and innovation suffer when employees are overwhelmed by complexity. In contrast, trusted leaders experience greater innovation and better performance. Yet only four in ten employees trust their boss. I view this as a huge gap that can potentially shrink when we reduce complexity.

Connect on a Basic Human Level

Some leading executives of highly innovative companies clearly understand the need to share their authentic selves as a way to build trust. In 2014, Apple CEO Tim Cook publicly came out in an opinion piece published in Bloomberg Businessweek. In an essay advocating for human rights, Cook said he set aside his privacy and publicly declared that he is gay in the hopes that he could help others who might be struggling.

Facebook's COO Sheryl Sandberg wrote movingly about her grief over the death of her husband Dave. In discussing her painful loss, she talked about how she decided to be open about her feelings with employees. "I realized that to restore that closeness with my colleagues that has always been so important to me, I needed to let them in," Sandberg wrote on Facebook, "And that meant being more open and vulnerable than I ever wanted to be. I told those I work with most closely that they could ask me their honest questions and I would answer. I also said it was okay for them to talk about how they felt."

Closer to home, our own SAP CEO Bill McDermott recently suffered an injury that led to the loss of his left eye. He reached out to SAP employees and spoke from the heart about the accident, his gratitude to family and colleagues, and his optimism about the future. SAP employees responded with heartfelt wishes for his recovery, many inspired by his willingness to be so open about such a tragic accident. The tragedy inspired him to increase his focus on individualized healthcare and the role SAP might play in making it better—and simpler—for people around the world.

Understand What "Simplifying Culture" Means

These executives turned difficult situations into opportunities to build trust. But you don't need a tragedy to begin simplifying your company culture. Why not consider ways to begin simplifying your corporate culture as one of your key 2016 initiatives?

Let's define our terms. A simplified corporate culture strives to:

- Do things in the way that creates the most value and engagement for all, with the least effort for all
- Make it easier for people to be their best and do great work

According to a report by The Jensen Group, a simpler environment gives employees the power to get their work done, to make a difference, and to control their own destiny. Simpler workplace cultures also make it easier for employees to do their best and be their best selves. But how can you create an ideal balance of deep trust, real inclusion, and maximum engagement within your organization?

Align and Commit to the Cause

Business leaders need to embrace the idea that ease of use and ease of effort can help create corporate return on investment. For example, at SAP, we have a shared aspiration to "make the world run better and improve people's lives." This is a bold but simple statement—and a sincere goal—that is at the heart of everything we do and every business decision we make. Our executives and leaders are unified behind this goal. It is repeated and shared often so there is no doubt about our commitment.

Ensuring that managers on the frontline understand their role in simplifying, communicating, and exemplifying the organization's messages and goals is critical. At SAP, we are proud of the training we offer to address the needs of those colleagues. There is often no greater representative of a group's goals than the manager with whom you interact on a day-to-day basis.

Design Everything to Be as Simple as Possible

Bill McDermott sets the tone for simplified communication—starting with our internal communication and meetings. He rarely relies on typical tools such as PowerPoint to share a message. Instead, Bill prefers to speak directly to audiences when possible (often via global broadcasts), engage in open Q&A sessions, or to send a simple one-paragraph mail—no "bells and whistles." We offer programs to help colleagues break messaging down to its most basic components, conduct "design thinking" training to enable out-of-the-box approaches to innovation, and encourage simple storytelling whenever possible. While there's still work to be done, I'm proud of my company's commitment to be more engaged "human to human" and less reliant on slides or fancy presentations that often complicate things.

Focusing on making things as simple as possible allows all of us to spend less time dealing with complexity and more time on the things that are truly important: connections, great work, and a better world.

HOW TO BUILD A GREAT WORKPLACE—FOR FREE

Jeffrey Hayzlett

Everyone is familiar with the culture that companies like Apple and Google have built in Silicon Valley. But not everyone can afford that "rock star" type of culture—and some might not even want it.

In Webster's dictionary, culture is "the integrated pattern of human knowledge, belief, and behavior that depends upon the capacity for learning and transmitting knowledge to succeeding generations."

In your workplace, culture is the everyday reality of organizational life. It is not the mission statement, your balance sheets, or even the employee handbook. The culture is what we do, what we say, the way we behave, and the way we treat each other. That encompasses everything from our products to our customers to our communities and even to ourselves.

As entrepreneurs, we left corporate America for a number of reasons, one of them being our dissatisfaction with the company's culture. We left to create something that fit our dreams, our persona, and our vision—our perfect corporate utopia.

How can we as business owners do that?

1. Start with Purpose

In the beginning, all that matters is building something great and lasting. When the head count is in the single digits, people discuss their soon-to-be culture around the table. Problems are still simple, and communication is direct. But as the company starts growing, communication becomes more sporadic (or non-existent), and consensus becomes harder to reach.

To avoid that scenario, have a purpose when you establish your new company's culture. To create that purpose, understand the "why" of the operation. What (or whom) does your business serve? Whatever your answer is, it should be authentic, inspirational, and aspirational. Companies with a strong purpose are well liked because they feel different (think Ikea or Apple).

Just don't think about copying these giants; no one likes a copycat. Instead, do what's right for your company. Think about what inspires you, and then execute it.

2. Create a Common Language, Values, and Standards

For a culture to be successful, those at your company must speak the same language and be on the same page about what your values are. This common language needs to be understood by everyone in the company—from the CEO down to the mail room worker. Write down those values. This makes them tangible, an essential element to make your culture withstand the test of time.

You must also have a common set of values—which are just your company's principles—and a common set of standards to measure how your principles are being upheld.

Only when you have aligned your language, values, and standards will you have a cohesive culture. Cohesiveness should be your end goal. It might seem tempting to employ a number of stop-gaps along the way, but that's only a short-term solution.

In order to create a long-lasting culture everyone understands, that culture will need to adapt as the company grows. Your core values are your constant staples, but the overall culture needs to be malleable enough to acclimate to different employees and changing times.

3. Lead by Example

A culture is shaped by how a company's leaders act. Every leader needs to internally and externally reflect the company's values and be its strongest advocates. They shouldn't recite the mission statement as a solution to everything but should exemplify what the company stands for.

Think about the Virgin brand and how Richard Branson embodies everything the company wants people to see them as: fun, bold, brash, and spirited. Leaders who exemplify incredible passion for what they do and have an exemplary work ethic are the main source of inspiration for other employees and those who want to join the company.

As a leader, you need to lead by example and be radically transparent. It won't matter one iota if you think you have a great culture yet your employees don't trust you. Being transparent, even when that's difficult, will go a long way in preserving the culture you originally envisioned.

4. Identify Your Ambassadors

Every company has them: employees who live, eat, and breathe your culture and help everyone else understand who you are as a company and what you stand for. These employees are your biggest advocates because they love the company almost as much as you do—they are your cheerleaders.

This type of employee is an invaluable asset. Once you identify who your cheerleaders are, ask them what they like about the current culture, what they don't like, and why culture matters to them. That will help you gauge if you should stay the course or make a few changes to the current culture.

The role of these ambassadors doesn't diminish with time. On the contrary, their role increases as your company grows and, in the end, gives you a competitive advantage. Why? Because customers will remember those who are positive and knowledgeable about the company (or brand) they represent.

5. Communicate Often and Honestly

Integrity has been defined as "doing the right thing, even when nobody's watching." Whatever you do, you must always demand that everyone in your company adhere to being truthful and approach everything with the utmost integrity. Failure to comply is not an option.

Part of being truthful as a leader is being completely honest about your strengths, weaknesses, and biases. It's pretty easy to boast about your talents, but don't think for a second you don't have any weaknesses--you do. This doesn't apply only to leadership but everyone.

As a leader, you must always communicate your values explicitly and continuously, internally and externally. Every employee must understand the culture and why it's important to preserve it. Self-awareness and communication will be essential when your culture isn't going all that well. Culture doesn't have to be a neatly wrapped package, but your communication and truthfulness must never waver. If people can't trust you, you don't have a leg to stand on.

6. Treat People Right

As a CEO or company leader, you need to treat your employees well. Otherwise, the culture you're trying to establish won't be of much use to you if you have a high turnover rate.

When you're thinking about hiring new employees, spend time screening for character rather than skill. Don't get me wrong: An impressive resume is something to be proud of, and it's important. But if your character is questionable, you're not a good fit for my company. Skills can be learned, but it's much harder to cultivate a good attitude and character.

Hiring someone with impressive skills and a bad attitude is a sure-fire way to sabotage your own culture, but once you've hired the right people, treat them right. Once you find someone with the right cultural fit, do everything in your power to develop them, and help that person scale.

You don't have to spend a fortune on an in-house sushi chef and a state-of-the-art office to create a great workplace. All six of these steps don't cost anything, and yet I know many people who would willingly trade their rock star work environment for a job in a company that embodied these traits.

14

THE COMPANY PEOPLE NEVER QUIT

Peter Daisyme

Having a high turnover rate as a result of employees quitting isn't exactly a great scenario for a business. As *The Wall Street Journal* notes:

> *High employee turnover hurts a company's bottom line. Experts estimate it costs upwards of twice an employee's salary to find and train a replacement. And churn can damage morale among remaining employees.*

How can you ensure that your employees won't leave you for someone else? I've found that it's all about company culture. With that in mind, here are some of the best ways to create a culture where employees will stick around for the long haul.

Make Sure Your Culture Matches the Work

Before you actually hire your first employee, you must have a clear understanding of what you and your business stands for. Once you identify that, you can construct a culture that will be conducive for the work your company does.

Take for example the open-source software company Red Hat. CEO Jim Whitehurst told Business Insider, "We built our culture to match open source's [culture]." Whitehurst goes on to explain, "The chaotic nature, the fact that people can call me up whenever and often call me an idiot to my face. We yell and we debate and we have these things out. Our culture matches the culture around open source, so the people who want to be involved in open source feel at home."

Hire the Right Employees Right from the Start

After you've created and identified your company culture, you can begin to find team members who match that environment. In fact, this may be one of the most important factors in reducing employee turnover.

A good example is Southwest Airlines as an organization who does this effectively by hiring employees based on attitude and not just skills. Southwest does this through recruitment ads by attracting people who are looking for and will fit well into the environment and dissuading those who would not be interested from applying.

With my own hosting company, I've hired the wrong person several times. They need to fit with every part of your company. Experience is good, but culture and meshing well is top priority with our company. This has led to a lot less people leaving.

Communicate and Be Transparent

As *Douglas* magazine states on TechVibes, "Employees want and need to know what is happening in your company. Tell the truth."

By keeping on an open line of communication with employees, you're helping to establish and maintain trust and respect, which you could do by publishing a weekly or monthly newsletter.

This not only includes answering any question or addressing any concerns, but it also means listening to what employees are saying. If there are rumors, address them openly. If there are any suggestions, take them into account. Not only will this keep employees happy, it could also reinforce the culture of your company.

Think More than Salary and Benefits

Salary and benefits play a big part in our company in making sure employees feel compensated. It's important to provide them with the proper compensation and benefits, and to communicate the potential for advancement. When you can't give high salaries, equity or stock may be something you can trade to make sure you have the best and brightest.

But a great workplace has to go further than a great compensation package. Employees are more likely to stay with a company with a positive work environment where they feel appreciated and cared for. This could mean offering a flexible schedule to help balance their personal and professional lives or creating opportunities for the entire team to have fun, such as having team activities.

Keeping the best employees is hard, but it's totally possible. Find what makes your startup culture work and what your employees need. This will lead to having a much healthier startup atmosphere while keeping employees working at your company!

ENTREPRENEUR VOICES SPOTLIGHT: INTERVIEW WITH JASON COHEN

Founder of WP Engine

Culture—By Choice or by Chance?

If there is such a thing, Jason Cohen is the archetype of an entrepreneur. He successfully built four tech startups from scratch. They run the gamut from bootstrapped to VC-funded and from solo ventures to partnerships. All of them broke at least a million in sales. Currently, he's the founder and CTO of WP Engine with over 500 employees and 5 percent of the digital world visiting a WP Engine site every day.

Unlike many entrepreneurs still in the trenches, Jason's had the luxury of being able to step away from not one, not two, but three of his businesses, plus being able to hand the CEO reins of his current business over to someone else. He's had the time to reflect back over his experience and put some deep thought into small business culture.

We get to reap the benefit.

Entrepreneur: Jason, talk to us about culture.

Cohen: Every company has a culture. The question is: did you decide what it was, or did it just emerge? Regardless, every organization has a personality and a value system. The way you observe that is through the behavior of the people in the organization.

When a business decision is difficult or unclear, how the organization handles it tells you what they value and how they think. The problem in a lot of companies is that those values emerge as a reaction to a situation instead of being something codified beforehand that they use as a guide when making those tough choices.

Entrepreneur: Was this your line of thinking in all your businesses?

Cohen: In my first three companies, I didn't care about any of this. I had the usual attitude of an entrepreneur—or at least a typical engineering-oriented entrepreneur—that all this culture stuff was just crap. "Who cares about all that? Even if there is such a thing as a company having a 'personality' of its own, I already know what it's going to be: as the founder, it's going to be mine."

In the beginning, that's roughly true. But the challenge is how that changes as things evolve. As you bring in more and more people, their personalities get infused into the company. If you hire people like you, then that reinforces the company looking like the founder. But if you hire people who aren't like you, then the company is going to look less like you.

And maybe that's a good thing, but whatever the case, you don't want your company to develop by accident. You want to be intentional about what it evolves into.

Entrepreneur: What changed your mind about culture?

Cohen: A talk by Michael Trafton at the Business of Software conference. It made me think that there might be other attributes that contribute to the success of a company besides how many lines of code you could write in a day.

It made me realize that, no matter what your position on this culture stuff was, you still had a culture at your company. If you're like I was, a skeptical, engineering-type founder, and say, "I don't care about all this touchy-feel stuff. It's all horseshit. All I care about are results and performance," even that is a statement of culture.

You're saying that you value one thing above another. You want results-driven people. So why wouldn't you hire accordingly? Why wouldn't you hire ambitious rock stars willing to work insane hours? Why would you hire someone who hates that kind of workplace? Why hire people who don't share your worldview?

There are certain things you can derive about the company's culture from someone who says they don't value "the culture stuff." You know it's probably a meritocracy. You know the sales force is probably quota-driven. You know the workplace is probably competitive and metric-driven. That's fine. There's nothing wrong with that. You just need to be clear that that's the kind of company you have so that you can find people who'll succeed in that kind of environment.

I know of a very successful, family-owned company that is 50 years old and does about $200 million in revenue a year. They're growing slowly but profitably. They don't have sales quotas because their culture is more around family, loyalty, and longevity. They've been successful following their model.

The laid-back, service-oriented salesperson at that family company won't succeed in the high-growth startup. The hard charging sales star at that startup will get frustrated by the slow pace and lack of opportunity to take down huge deals and make tons of money at the family company. Neither is right or wrong, but one person isn't going to be successful in a company culture that runs counter to their own values.

In retrospect, I can look back over my other three companies and see those problems now. I used to ask myself, "Why did this person not work out? And why did it take us a year-and-a-half to figure that out?" or, "Why was this so difficult? We just kept going around and around." The fundamental problem in those situations was that we didn't have common ground. We valued different things which means that we had different priorities and made different decisions. Looking back, it's clear now why we kept having problems: their worldview didn't work in a company that ran counter to it.

Entrepreneur: You've obviously put a lot of thought into this. What about the dangers of hiring people who think like you? At what point is too much of a good thing not a good thing?

Cohen: You want diversity in some things. At WP Engine, for example, we're one of the most diverse tech companies I know of. Over half of our executive team are women, for example. That kind of diversity is important.

But something that you should not be diverse in are your values. At WP Engine, we have a certain way we think about accountability, trust, and empowerment; we don't want variation in those things. We want shared beliefs. If someone fundamentally disagrees with the things we value, then they're not a fit.

Entrepreneur: Last words of advice to entrepreneurs?

Cohen: At no time in this conversation did I mention a plan. I didn't talk about the future. I didn't mention milestones. I never used the word "goals."

Some entrepreneurs say you need a plan; some say the future's so uncertain that you can't plan for it. I don't care either way. What you do have to do is decide what's important. Be explicit about those things so that when you have to make a hard decision in a complex situation that doesn't have a clear answer, you're deciding around what's important to you.

If you want to make as much money as possible, then if that's true, own it! Align yourself around that and optimize your company for that so that it's more likely to come true than if you try to get there by accident. If you're not honest with yourself about what's important to you, then you'll only reach it by random chance--if it all. That's stupid.

Whatever you are, be intentional about it.

PART II
LEADING—REFLECTIONS

The interview with the founder of WP Engine brings this section full circle to the opening of its first chapter: as the entrepreneur, you are already setting the culture of your company. The only question is whether you're purposeful or passive about it. Put another way, are you letting the workplace form by itself—or are you deliberately leading it towards the vision you have for it?

Lee Iacocca once wrote, "Sometimes even the best manager is like the little boy with the big dog, waiting to see where the dog wants to go so that he can take him there."

Perhaps that's the difference between a leader and a manager. If you simply manage your company, it will take on a life of its own. Leading, on the other hand, takes effort, intention, and consistency.

But to lead means that someone must follow. Harkening back to the reflection on clarity: if people are going to follow you, they need to believe in you, in the company, and in your vision. Ideally, you don't just want followers—you want *believers*.

As Jeffrey Hayzlett said, when your company grows, those who believe in you and your vision will become the ambassadors of your culture—not just to new employees, but to customers, vendors, investors, competitors, and anyone else who watches your company. They'll become the champions of "how we do things around here." They're going to follow your lead and model their expectations from your actions. Make sure you're modeling what you want to see.

TOOLS AND TACTICS

"Leading change" is all well and good, but . . . the devil's in the details.

If you're serious about creating an incredible culture, you can't stop at the high-level ideas; you have to delve into the tools and tactics that support your aim. Fortunately, our contributors are as prolific of writers about the "how" as they are about the "why."

Like the previous section, most of the advice in this one is free or nearly free to put into practice. In fact, as the article on compensation points out, there's only a correlation between salary and employee satisfaction up to a point. After that, money's not much of a motivating factor.

Another thing that some of our contributors also seem to despise: ping pong tables. Not that they're necessarily against them, but they hate when people use them in place of meaningful efforts. (Really hate them. As in, we had to edit out a lot of "ping pong tables" throughout this book.)

Instead, the tools and tactics outlined here are more along the lines of "praise someone publicly" or "allow anonymous feedback." If those seem simplistic, perhaps that's the point: entrepreneurial culture as a whole has gotten so focused on the perks of a great workplace—and especially in startup culture— that it's neglected attending to the basics, like the trinity of respect, credibility, and fairness the CEO of Great Place to Work Michael Bush spoke about.

Additionally, not all businesses can readily afford the "paid" vacations or other such real costs earlier contributors spoke about. Plenty of small business owners sweat about meeting payroll on Friday, never mind taking the entire company on a retreat.

That's one of the reasons why the lion's share of this section focuses on low- to no-cost ways to shape your culture. They're things virtually every entrepreneur can do at every size and in every industry.

They've made it easy. It's up to you to do the hard part of putting it to work.

15

TOOLS TO SHAPE YOUR CULTURE

Nadya Khoja

Ping pong tables and "Scotch Fridays" don't lead to success and growth.

Sure, these are nice benefits to have, but in the long run, they will just lead to a more complacent staff—a group confused about what the actual values and goals of the business are.

What many CEOs and VPs struggle to accomplish is identifying what exactly "culture" means and why it's important. There are a few things you can do to start focusing on improving your culture and using it as a tool to boost productivity, find top talent, and accelerate growth.

Be Explicit about What Matters

Core values are essentially a deeper look into the behaviors of a company and specifically the behaviors that lead to success. Jocelyn Goldfein of Zetta Venture Partners says "culture is the behavior you reward and punish."

How often do new employees make their way into a company already understanding the culture? Not often. It takes time for new hires to get their bearings and fit in. What do they do instead? They look around and try to mimic what other people are doing—specifically, what the top performers are doing.

Here is an exercise you can do during your next team meeting. Ask everyone what it takes to be successful at your company. Write down the responses. These are the behaviors that your business rewards and, in turn, the values you promote. Next, make a list of these values and ask your team to describe what it means to demonstrate those values, using specific examples.

For example, Venngage has five main core values that make a great employee:

1. You own your job.
2. You reflect, plan, and act.
3. You continuously improve.
4. You're a team player.
5. You create great customer experiences.

Although these values describe *what* it is we look for in employees, they fail to address *how* to demonstrate each core value. It's extremely important that your staff understands the how, which is why you must go through each value and ask your team how they would demonstrate it. For instance, when I asked the marketing team how to "own their jobs" as marketers, they came up with the following list:

- Staying on top of trends in the industry and hot topics
- Knowing what strengths you bring to the team and capitalizing on that
- Being open to learning new things
- Taking accountability for your own actions
- Being proactive/taking initiative
- Presenting the company to others positively (brand evangelism)
- Striving to become a thought leader
- Staying on top of deadlines
- Constantly working towards becoming a well-rounded marketer

So, how do you get people to embody those behaviors?

Measure Values vs. Behavior

In Gino Wickman's book *Traction: Get a Grip on Your Business*, he talks about an evaluation process called "The People Analyzer." This process is first and foremost designed to clarify whether or not you have the right person in the right role. The secondary purpose is to identify if the members on your team do, in fact, demonstrate the company's core values.

Here is what it looks like:

Name	Own Your Job	Create Great Customer Experiences	Reflect, Plan, and Act	Continuous Improvement	Win Together, Lose Together
John	−	−	−	−	−
Linda	+/−	+/−	+/−	+/−	+/−
Alice	+	+	+	+	+

The scale is easy to follow. A minus sign means the person does not reflect that behavior, a plus sign means they do, and a plus/minus sign means that they kind of embody the value but aren't where they should be.

Get Serious About Enforcing Culture

Every 30 days, use the people analyzer to "grade" each of your employees. If they underperform in a certain area, be sure that you bring up the issue. Let them know that you will check in again in 30 days. This is their first strike.

After another 30 days, if they are still underperforming, go over the issues once more during your one-on-one. What specifically are they doing wrong? Where are they falling short? Be specific. Then, give them another 30 days to get up to speed. This is strike two.

If after another 30 days the minus sign is still holding strong, it is unlikely that the employee will improve. This is the point when you should let them go. This is strike three.

Reward Embodying Culture

Like I mentioned before, new employees—or existing ones for that matter—will mimic good behavior. If they see that one particular employee gets along well with the boss, that their opinions are always heard, and that they are awarded exciting opportunities, others will try to follow their patterns.

To clarify your culture and help others embody it, reward behaviors that reflect the culture. At Venngage, we give "shout outs" to A-players every week during our team meetings. For instance, if Alice took initiative to attend a meetup on growth marketing during the weekend, that is a prime example of demonstrating the core value of "continuous improvement."

Envision the Greater Goal

As a CEO, you have an agenda—a greater goal you want to achieve. What is that goal? I'll tell you now it shouldn't be revenue driven. Revenue should be a side effect of hitting that goal.

Some might assume that a CEO's goal is the mission statement of the company, but this is not entirely accurate. The mission statement is the company goal, but your goal as a CEO needs to be more personal. There's a more pointed question that might lead you towards better understanding what that goal is: how do you want to be remembered? What do you want the words on your tombstone to read?

It's important that you figure out the answer to this because it's what will guide the values that make up the culture of your company, and in turn, lead to your success. Culture can make or break a company. Do not be the person who puts your product above your culture. Instead, focus on providing meaning to the work your employees do.

YOU CAN'T BUY HAPPINESS— YOURS OR THEIRS

John Rampton

A high salary, large bonuses, and frequent raises are often used as incentives to make employees happy. Here's the thing: Money isn't the silver bullet to employee happiness.

Take the infamous case of Gravity Payments. In 2015, the company made international headlines when it raised the minimum salary of their employees to $70,000 a year, to be implemented over the next three years. Initially, employees were ecstatic. However, there was also a fair amount of backlash from employees. In fact, two employees quit over the raise.

Employee Maisey McMaster was on board at first and loved the culture. After devoting five years working her way up to financial advisor, she was bothered by the raise. "He gave raises to people who have the least skills and are the least equipped to do the job, and the ones who were taking on the most didn't get much of a bump," Ms. McMaster's said. In her opinion, it would have been more fair to issue smaller increases with the opportunity to earn a future raise after they gained more experience.

This is just one example where raises don't create happiness. If money doesn't make employees happy, then what, exactly, does? And why is that such a big deal?

Money Can't Buy Happiness

While pay does factor into whether or not an employee joins or sticks with a company, there are many influences that determine happiness. Dr. Andrew Chamberlin, chief economist and director of research at Glassdoor, wrote in the *Harvard Business Review*:

> *One of the most striking results we've found is that, across all income levels, the top predictor*

of workplace satisfaction is not pay. It is the culture and values of the organization, followed closely by the quality of senior leadership and the career opportunities at the company. Among the six workplace factors we examined, compensation and benefits were consistently rated among the least important factors of workplace happiness.

A 2010 study from Princeton that found that "having a higher income increases happiness but only up to about $75,000 per year." After that, "higher pay doesn't influence happiness much, and other factors take over."

Money in your bank doesn't mean happiness, but Chamberlin's research found that either pay or compensation is "still the top factor that job seekers consider when evaluating potential employers."

To attract top talent, employers have to offer competitive pay and benefits. Ultimately, though, Chamberlin and Glassdoor found that culture and the values of the organization are the largest predictor of employee satisfaction, followed by senior leadership, career opportunities, business outlook, and work-life balance.

It should be noted that compensation and benefits, work-life balance, and business outlook for the company become less important as pay rises. After a point, the data shows overall that compensation and benefits is among the least important workplace factors.

Why is happiness such a big deal, anyway?

Happy employees are 12 percent more productive while unhappy employees are 10 percent less productive. Additionally, companies with happy employees can outperform their competitors by 20 percent.

Still not convinced? Happier employees are more sociable and generous, as well as more energetic and healthy. Happy employees take far fewer sick days than unhappy employees. Employee morale impacts productivity and your bottom line. The CDC reported in 2015 that worker illness and injury cost U.S. employers more than $225 billion annually—or $1,685 per employee.

So, how can you keep your employees happy?

Start with the Person in the Mirror

A sure-fire way to have a happier team is to become a better manager. Lead by example. Show you care that everyone is satisfied by starting to communicate more effectively and providing performance evaluation feedback. Stay on schedule, using automation, and collaborating with your team.

Get to Know Your Team

Remember, your employees are all unique and have different happiness triggers. Even though raises may not make everyone happy, it could work for an employee or two. Spend time actually getting to know your team so that you can identify what's going to make those specific people happy.

Hire employees who are a good fit for your culture and remove toxic personalities already on staff. Acknowledge and celebrate accomplishments together, encourage workplace friendships, and provide comfy furniture. Design the office for maximum productivity. Just remember: even though you want the workplace to be fun, don't force it on your employees.

Make Work-life Balance a Priority

Offering more vacation time and flexible hours is a good first step. Employees are also looking for organizations that intentionally blur the lines between life and work. For example, Eventbrite is considered "one of the happiest places we've ever seen" by Business Insider because the company allows employees to bring their dogs to work. The company also lets employees meditate whenever they want, and go bowling during lunch.

Besides the basic benefits, you can offer employees ancillary benefits, such as dental, optical, and wellness. Add health-related perks like gym memberships or quiet spaces for employees to take a nap or meditate. You can also provide healthy snacks or the option to occasionally work from home.

Focus on Developing Your People

Training opportunities and career mentoring are often used to retain employees. The problem is that it will do the opposite if they can't climb the corporate ladder. To counter this, businesses should have regular career planning discussions with their employees.

Go a step further: include employees in the decision-making process. This makes them feel like they're VIPs since they're involved with helping the business grow. It also shows that their work and feedback is making a difference.

Focus on the Important Things--Not the Trivial

Achievement and recognition will always motivate your employees and put a smile on their face. Again, if you get to know your individual team members, you can give them rewards that they actually want. At the same, everyone loves receiving a shout-out and a simple "thank you." Simply put, show your gratitude, and always treat your team with respect.

Happiness should be a goal for business leaders across the board. At the same time, it's important that you understand that happiness is a product of your company's culture.

That means allowing dogs in the workplace, having ping-pong tournaments, and free professional development classes won't resolve all of your major underlying problems. Instead, create a culture where employees have the opportunity to connect, learn, and grow.

17

BOOTSTRAP YOUR CULTURE

Kelly Lovell

A strong team culture is an integral part of successful ventures. A motivated team can translate into better work productivity, increased product quality, enhanced customer support, and overall office spirit.

Benefits like these are the reasons that the best places to work are those that foster team culture. (Work-life balance and a healthy work environment are close seconds.)

For examples, consider a list titled "Baltimore's Best Places to Work in 2015." The list's winners featured such perks as bring your pet to work day, paintball outings, and office gyms.

Similarly, free daily lunches, volunteer days, and family games were shared themes among *Crain's New York Business'* 2015 "Best Places to Work in NYC."

As these lists revealed, your team builds the foundation for your culture to grow and sets the overall tone. But if you try to build a structure on soft ground, it will likely fail. And starting a company with a weak team culture and scale has the same result. A strong, sturdy culture for your team established from the beginning will determine your company's overall tone.

But creating a prosperous team can be tough during your company's initial growth stages, or worse, when it's in bootstrapping mode. So how do you foster team spirit on a startup budget? Here are five quick, practically free ideas you can employ to build positive team spirit.

1. Homemade Surprises

As Jim Rohn said, "Time is more valuable than money. You can get more money, but you cannot get more time." In a similar vein, nothing says appreciation quite like the boss taking that time to make homemade cookies or cupcakes for the team. Home-baked goods not only reflect extra care but can be surprisingly cheaper than store-bought goods (and much tastier). So, be creative. Bake or cook up your favorite dish for a snack or lunch, and share it with your team.

2. Group Crafts

Even those who are not overly creative can benefit from activities that promote self-expression. Art therapy has proven therapeutic benefits for individuals experiencing illness, trauma, and mental health struggles. It also has a professional application: art helps professionals achieve personal insight, resolve conflicts, improve interpersonal skills, and, most importantly, reduces negative stress. All of this combines to foster an enhanced workplace culture.

Consider offering an interactive crafting activity to your team. For Halloween, I hosted a pumpkin-carving contest at my office. I picked up some fun decorations and paint from a dollar store along with a few pumpkins and carving materials from home. Then, we all had fun seeing the final masterpieces take shape. Whether the context is an office decorating party, a vision board creation, or a holiday-themed activity, group crafts are a fun way to inspire your team members and learn more about them.

3. Game Night

Play can lead to more creative and adaptable workers. In *Response of the Brain to Enrichment*, neuroscience researcher Marian Diamond described how "enriched," playful environments powerfully shape the cerebral cortex, the area of the brain where the highest cognitive processing takes place.

Diamond concluded,

> *There are measurable benefits to enriching [making playful] an individual's environment in whatever terms that individual perceives his immediate environment as enriched.*

Some companies have taken note: Apple, Zappos, Twitter, and Google are just a few of the corporate leaders that have adopted this playful attitude in the workplace. When I visited Google headquarters, for instance, Lego bins were plentiful, followed by Foosball tables, giant slides, and a variety of games for employees.

You don't need Google's budget to tap into these benefits of play. Hosting a game night is sure to inspire your team's creative spirit. Grab a deck of cards and chips for a fun poker night, or better yet, have each of your team members bring their favorite game to your party. Games are an effective way to relieve stress, promote team conversation, and inspire team spirit.

4. Motivational Content

According to a 2013 *State of the Global Workplace* study from Gallup, only 13 percent of employees surveyed worldwide considered themselves to be engaged. The bulk of "unengaged" employees, meanwhile, indicates a lack of motivation in the work environment. An occasional inspirational quote or message to your team is an affordable idea that can go a long way to improving employee motivation and commitment to your company.

As this same study showed, 67 percent of employees surveyed reported feeling engaged when their managers focused on positive characteristics. To tap into this insight, reflect on what personally motivates you.

Do you have favorite quotes, TEDtalks, music, articles, books, or videos that inspire you? Share that content with your team. A simple quote emailed at the start of the day or a funny photo at the end of a long day's work can help keep spirits high and create a positive team mood.

5. Recognition

Recognition is the best way to make your team feel valued and appreciated, which in turn will build your company's progress. As an American Psychological Association Harris Interactive 2012 Workplace Survey indicated, employees who reported feeling valued were also 60 percent more likely to do their very best for their employers.

Fortunately, recognition need not be an expensive proposition. While employee incentives are part of a $100-plus billion industry, non-cash incentives make up 46 percent. Verbal recognition and a pat on the back can go a long way. A recognition strategy could be as simple as sending a shout-out on Friday to recognize a member's progress or emailing a quick digital card to the "team member of the month."

These small gestures not only show that you care about and value your team's efforts, they can enhance your team's self-confidence. The key to building team culture is to remember that your foundation is built on attitude and motivation. Activities that enhance self-esteem, promote expression, and create positive memories contribute to your overall team spirit.

YOUR PEOPLE AREN'T AS HAPPY AS YOU THINK

Heather R. Huhman

When VitalSmarts surveyed 1,200 employees from various companies on workplace culture, it found that many employers were missing the mark. While leaders want to believe they've created environments filled with innovation and teamwork, there's a good chance their employees see the workplace as one of obedience, competition, and predictability. Let's contrast this ideal against what employees really think, and then look at how to close the gap.

The Ideal

As you climb the corporate ladder, the comments about a company's culture become more and more positive. These leaders dream of a workplace full of innovation; they believe they've provided the necessary tools for employees to move successfully forward. They make sure that new methods are always being created to better the work process for employees.

These visions of an ideal workplace include a culture of teamwork where employees are on the same page and working together in a productive manner. In this world, there's no such thing as generational gaps because a company's employees will all have the same training and correct amount of knowledge to complete their daily tasks.

The Reality

Unfortunately, the happiness that employers believe their employees experience isn't their employees' reality. Globoforce conducted a survey of more than 800 full-time U.S. employees and found that 47 percent of its respondents did not feel their company leaders cared about or actively tried to create a great workplace.

Maybe employers should consider a reality check: their employees are dealing with the reality of miscommunication, technology advancements and challenges, and the ever-changing nature of work. These issues, combined with the overwhelming feeling of leaders not actively trying to better the work culture, create frustration and lead to decreased productivity.

Generational gaps create tension within the ideal teamwork vision. Employees from different age segments view the nature of work differently and place different values on various workplace benefits. Unify surveyed 9,000 knowledge workers and found that 16- to 24-year-olds described the ideal workplace as creative, successful, and exciting. In contrast, 35- to 44-year-olds wanted to be part of a workplace that is creative, successful, and supportive.

With one generation looking for excitement in the workplace and another seeking support, the lines get blurred with employees understanding one another when they work together. This type of miscommunication can damper employee happiness and production.

Feeling that the proper tools aren't being delivered or updated can push a company's culture into a frustrating, unproductive standstill. Companies with outdated technology, as well as those with newer technology but no ongoing training on it, are hurting themselves and their employees. Innovation and growth can't happen if employees are dealing with such hindering issues.

The Bridge

To keep current employees happy and productive, understand how employees view your culture. Give them specific goals, assure them that their frustrations are heard and addressed, and institute employee reviews.

In this context, performance-management tools like Reflektive enable real-time feedback, performance reviews, and goal alignment. Listening—and really hearing—any feedback employees have gives employers a view of reality they may not have otherwise. This new online vantage point helps employers draw a new roadmap for workplace culture.

Performance reviews in particular help employees stay connected with employers about their progress. Innovation increases when employees completely understand what needs improving. Separate reviews for each employee are important because everyone feels their performance is being reviewed from a range of job responsibilities.

Aligning goals in weekly meetings is another step. Goal-setting can begin the process of closing the generational gap by encouraging teamwork. Encourage goal-setting that includes all generations' point of view to bring the team closer together. For example, create guidelines that will make a task "exciting" for the younger generation and line up tools to help everyone show "support" for the older generation.

Discover what matters most to your people, and deliver it.

HOW GOOGLE REINVENTED THE EMPLOYEE SURVEY

Steffen Maier

Ever since the term "employee engagement" started being widely used in the 1990s, it's been hailed as the key to high productivity and retention, profit increase, and better customer satisfaction. Companies took notice of the benefits and sought to turn this abstract concept into a trackable metric. Many companies began administering annual employee-satisfaction surveys.

These snapshots help companies check in with team members and assess how happy their employees are in the workplace. While the practice now is widespread, some thought leaders in human resources have begun questioning the annual survey's accuracy and usefulness.

The Problem with Most Feedback Tools

How do you know the answers you're getting are valid in terms of what you're trying to achieve? A survey by Impact Achievement Group and HRmarketer discovered 48 percent of all respondents did not believe employee surveys provide an honest and accurate assessment, compared to 31 percent who thought surveys painted a true picture.

Some argue that employees are more apt to answer survey questions positively—creating a sense that everything seems fine (at least on the surface). Employees who give falsely high marks might fear retaliation or feel a general disinterest toward a survey that takes time out of their busy work day. Others might believe their answers won't make a difference. This sense of apathy is evidenced by the simple fact that many companies have trouble achieving high participation rates.

Here's the most revealing finding from the Achievement Group/HRmarketer study: 58 percent of respondents agreed that results did not—or only slightly did—help managers gain a better understanding of what behaviors or practices they could change to improve. If surveys don't yield any actionable information, will their results make any difference in how a workplace is run? This loop perpetuates the apathy problem. If employees are conditioned to believe they won't see actual changes in their work environments, what incentive do they have to fill out a satisfaction survey?

A recent LinkedIn post from *Forbes* writer Liz Ryan had some pretty harsh words about employee-satisfaction surveys:

> *Employee Engagement Surveys are the business equivalent of giving the prisoners in a penitentiary a survey to complete once a year and slide through the bars of their cells. The survey process cements an unequal power relationship.*

Is she right? Are engagement surveys an HR check-off box at the least—and a tool for damage control at most? Do these surveys simply give employees the pretense of a voice within a company? Maybe it's time to rethink employee-satisfaction surveys and how we administer them.

How Google Does It Differently

At Google, surveys aren't just about checking the pulse of the workplace; they're about constantly striving to improve it. The company's People Operations team (formerly known as HR) uses feedback to optimize different aspects of its people processes and align them with its unique work culture. As a result, the company reports an average participation rate of 90 percent.

Nearly every decision the company takes is data driven—and that's representative of the culture in a majority engineer workforce, too. But the very nature of the HR field focuses on interpersonal relationships in the workplace. It can be difficult to assess based on pure input/output metrics alone. Productivity metrics are extremely important to gauge effectiveness, but they don't tell the whole story.

For this reason, Google integrates the human aspects through use of people analytics. Mixing quantitative and qualitative data enables leaders to really dig deep into the company's inner-culture dynamics. Google has used people analytics to improve the workplace across a number of studies.

Project Oxygen

Through surveys, company leaders learned that most Googlers are averse to hierarchy. Many employees—

cofounders Larry Page and Sergey Brin among them—questioned the need for a management level. They thought they simply might flatten the company structure. First, though, they engaged the company's people analytics team to determine whether having managers makes a real difference.

In a 2008 study, Project Oxygen, People Operations workers analyzed managers' performance ratings and the upward feedback gathered in employee surveys. They then compared these results with productivity metrics. The outcome? At Google, great managers lead to more engaged and productive teams.

The people analytics team took the research a step further to identify which characteristics made a great manager. The team returned to comments from surveys, performance evaluations, and great-manager nominations. They then conducted double-blind interviews with the company's highest- and lowest-rated managers.

Rather than prove managers unnecessary, Project Oxygen discovered mid-level leaders were essential to create conditions in which other employees could thrive. To be truly effective, though, the company had to turn away from supervisory tactics that ran counter to what Googlers need from a manager. Micromanaging was at the top of the list.

Google turned Project Oxygen's findings into the company's Top 8 management behaviors and now uses the list as a guidebook to identify and train leaders from within Google's ranks. The initiative's data-based roots make it easier for managers to accept these standards and move toward meeting expectations.

Project Aristotle

In a 2012 study code-named Project Aristotle, Google sought the perfect formula for creating effective teams. Leaders looked at each team's performance metrics and then at perceptions of effectiveness itself. People analytics acknowledges that abstract terms mean different things to different people. Through Project Aristotle, Google learned that executives equated effectiveness with productivity. For employees, team culture was the most important measure of effectiveness. Meanwhile, team leaders ranked ownership, vision, and goals as the most important influences.

To capture these varied factors, the people analytics team examined qualitative surveys from the three major employee groups and compared the information to sales performances (stacked against quarterly quota). Combining human experience with hard data allowed Google to see which teams fared the best. Even more important, the results helped Google understand why certain teams succeeded. These findings formed the basis of Google's five essential factors to create a positive work environment.

Learning from Google

Google's process provides HR insights into employee engagement. It also creates trust between employer and employee. Googlers feel a sense of equality because they directly shape how their company is run.

Laszlo Bock, Google's former Head of People Operations, described the strategy in a recent *Harvard Business Review* article. His piece listed four steps leaders can take to "move from hunches to science" in their own decision-making processes. Bock:

- asks employees to identify the company's most pressing people issues;
- asks employees to suggest ways to improve;
- encourages the analytics team to share feedback company-wide;
- empowers leaders to run experiments that test which data-supported theories work best.

It's impossible to overstate the importance of engaging the human aspect in HR efforts. Pure performance data alone isn't enough. Qualitative results help leaders truly understand the underlying dynamics at work in their companies. Done right, employee surveys play a crucial role. Start by asking what workers want to improve, and take the next steps to move forward from there.

20

FEEDBACK THAT BUILDS CULTURE

Sujan Patel

In the early days of her consultancy career, IBM performance marketing expert Jackie Bassett was assigned to a project that, as she wrote, she "didn't like very much." She was obliged to work crazy hours alongside a demoralized team with minimal instruction on the expectations of her role.

Although Bassett knew deep down that her performance wasn't up to scratch, no one said anything. It wasn't until her written performance evaluation—handed to her more than a month after the project ended—that she realized her superiors were unhappy with her work.

Bassett was left wondering, *Why didn't [they] say anything?*

Sadly, this is far from an isolated incident. It's not unusual for companies to provide scheduled feedback—such as when a project wraps up, or during a yearly review—yet fail to offer it when it's needed most and is most valuable: in real time.

Don't reserve feedback for "special occasions" like yearly reviews or the point at which something's gone wrong or spectacularly right. A simple "great job on xyz today" will go a long way toward boosting morale and creating a workplace in which feedback becomes part of the culture.

In fact, employees who receive regular feedback have been shown to work harder, be more engaged, and offer greater loyalty to their employers. The most successful companies have built a strong culture of feedback by making it a normal, everyday part of company life.

What are the best practices in these places?

Don't Put Too Much Stock in Performance Reviews

In an interview, Bill Sims, the author of *Green Beans & Ice Cream*, described how Microsoft had ended the use of a system known as "forced rankings." Part of performance reviews, forced rankings used a scoring system to identify the best- and worst-performing employees. The worst-performing employees might then be fired.

The problem with such a system (aside from its glaring brutality) is that performance reviews tend to focus on isolated examples of each employee's work. They're often carried out by top-level management with little, if any, direct contact with their employees' day-to-day performance. Instead, those managers rely on third-party reports from lower management and team leaders.

In short: performance reviews are ineffective at improving performance.

Instead, the way to go is to empower and encourage those who work directly with your staff. In this way, you can appraise and praise employees' work as it happens.

Separate Positive and Negative Feedback

A popular management strategy is to cushion the blow of negative feedback by wrapping it in positivity. This is more commonly known as the "sandwich approach."

At first glance, the sandwich approach seems logical. It certainly feels like the kinder way of delivering bad news, but in the long run, it devalues positive feedback. If you need to address poor performance, focus on the issue at hand. Likewise, offer positive feedback when it's called for. Don't ever "save it" in order to soften its bad-news component. Research has shown that aspects of both positive and negative feedback are best shared as soon as possible.

Give More Good Feedback Than Bad

Both positive and negative feedback are very important. Positive feedback helps boost staff morale while negative feedback allows you to address problems head-on. Both forms of feedback serve to improve performance.

That said, a staff member receiving so much negative feedback that it outweighs the positive will understandably start to feel its brunt. If this happens, chances are there are one of two issues at play:

1. A genuine problem with the staff member's performance
2. A problem with management's approach to feedback

The first example is a separate issue unlikely to be resolved solely by feedback of any sentiment. The second example is the fault of management, which needs to overhaul its approach to ensure that positive feedback significantly outweighs the negative. How "significantly" should that be?

Research conducted by academic expert Emily Heaphy and consultant Marcial Losada in 2013 found that the average ratio of positive to negative comments for the highest-performing teams included in the study was 5.6.

That is, for every negative comment, there were nearly six positive ones.

They Use Trust as the Bedrock of Feedback

An effective culture of feedback has to be built on trust. If your staff members don't trust one another—or even you—how can you expect them to take feedback seriously?

To get around this, Shopify CEO Tobi Lütke implemented a system called the "trust battery." He's explained that the trust battery is,

> charged at 50 percent when people are first hired. And then every time you work with someone at the company, the trust battery between the two of you is either charged or discharged, based on things like whether you deliver on what you promise.

The concept stems from the fact that humans already work that way; the battery simply serves as a metaphor. It helps to strengthen the impact of another system that's unique to Shopify: an internal wiki that openly displays each employee's strengths and weaknesses. The wiki helps accelerate the process of learning about colleagues and how they work best (and how best to work with them). It's a great idea, but one that can only work under a culture of complete openness and trust.

It also explains why Google executive Larry Page can get away with "bursting into a room and making a big show of announcing that a set of ads sucked."

Most execs would terrify their employees with such an outburst, but Google has spent so long building an open, communicative culture of trust that in this context, it works.

In all these examples, feedback is embedded in the companies' overall culture. Just as importantly, feedback supports and reinforces their cultures instead of demoralizing their employees or eroding the workplace environment.

Can your business say the same?

EIGHT EASY TACTICS TO MAKE WORK FUN AND PRODUCTIVE

Peter Daisyme

Companies want machine-like levels of productivity because they know that the science of productivity—the ability to output—can make a significant difference to the bottom line of any company.

However, there is also an art to productivity—that is, the ability to figure out how to not only do more but to make "more" better at the same time. It's also important to remember that even machines break down as parts wear out over time without regular maintenance.

The same goes with the talent you have in your workplace. Your employees can be efficient machines when given the right maintenance, the occasional tune-up, and some tactics designed to keep fueling their desire to deliver maximum quality output.

Since having employees, I've learned a lot about ways to continue increasing their productivity at work—even achieving greater output of up to 20 percent. Here are eight tips you can put to work in your business that are proven ways to drive greater productivity in the workplace.

1. Encourage with Words

When you tell someone what a great job they are doing and recognize that they are already working hard, you will get even more out of them. That's because you make them feel good when you acknowledge their efforts, and that, in turn, makes them want to do more so there is an opportunity for future compliments.

I have found that verbal encouragement goes farther than even money in terms of motivation. I try to always have an actual incident or example where this employee has a noteworthy accomplishment. Even when I have talented people outside of the office on a remote basis, I regularly thank them for their great work and continually cheer them on. They feel good, and so do I. It's positively invigorating for all involved.

2. Reward Through Healthy Competition

Being highly competitive, I've found that the normal rewards and incentives are not enough. Instead, I found value in creating healthy competitions among the staff or teams. For certain projects or targets, I have created competitions to see which team or individual can meet the objectives first or achieve the greatest number of criteria. The person or team that does then receives some type of reward, which has been anything from a paid day off to gift cards to lunch out with me.

3. Drive Accountability and Sense of Ownership

When my staff knows that "it's on them" and that there are consequences if they don't get a project done, I find that they pick up the pace more so than if I hadn't driven the accountability point home. The idea here is not to scare them into thinking they will lose their jobs. When delegating, I don't lead by fear. Instead, I use these opportunities as a place to illustrate their ownership in the company and that, if they do well and take responsibility for our results, then there will be rewards for them and for everyone.

This doesn't always mean expecting accountability—it often means allowing accountability. The drivers want the responsibility and accountability. In doing so, I see much more meticulous attention to even the smallest details related to a project, resulting in fewer mistakes and more efficient work.

4. Make It Fun

While I do like to work hard, I also like to play hard. That's why we have been known to take a break to get out of the office and go for a walk or head somewhere to unwind for a bit.

For all of us, this has helped to clear the mind and refocus. The result has been more work completed at a faster, higher quality rate. This also bonds those in the office, and they look out for each other and lift the value of all employees work.

5. Set Social Media and Phone Policies

I've had to set some guidelines through a formal social media and phone policy to ensure we (including myself!) are not distracted by electronic devices or social channels. Instead, I have designated certain times of the day for these diversions because I understand that everyone likes to stay in touch with their friends and family as well as maybe even stay up to date on the latest funny pet videos or their Words with Friends games. However, by setting some boundaries on use, I've regained the staff's attention and channeled that into greater productivity.

6. Challenge

There's nothing like giving workers something new to do outside of their comfort zone. It certainly wakes them up as their existing knowledge and skills go to work to figure out how to tackle a new project and do it well. Rather than shutting down out of fear, I have found greater enthusiasm from my staff when I throw them a curve ball like learning a new software or tool or maybe even handing them a task well outside anything they have ever done before. They are nervous but excited, and that translates into greater productivity, especially as their learning curve catches up.

7. Minimize Meetings

I have found myself rolling my eyes at the thought of another meeting. No one really likes them, and most people's minds are somewhere else in the midst of the meeting. That's why I keep office meetings and conference calls to a bare minimum. Whether it's setting a timer and encouraging staff to keep it as brief as possible, taking the meeting outdoors on the urban hiking trail near our office, or just simply taking care of many meeting-related tasks through online collaboration tools, I have discovered that the time not in a meeting is being spent on many more productive activities.

8. Aim for Comfort

Too hot, too cold, too stuffy, too drafty, or too much of anything and a person will find themselves easily distracted. Finding that optimum temperature and airflow for the office may sound trivial, but something this simple and easy to fix can make an extraordinary difference.

When my staff is working in a cool (but not too cold!) office, they are more alert and focused on their projects. However, if the temperature gets too hot and there is no airflow, I immediately see the difference in their demeanor, like they all could use a nap—although the idea of sleep pods for power naps is still on my list of potential productivity strategies.

I have also seen an increase in personal power as I have allowed others to be in charge of their own level of comfort. A small space heater here or there or a fan lets the employees know that I understand there are differences in personal comfort and I respect that.

Besides these strategies, research has uncovered additional ways to boost productivity by up to 15 percent while also reducing operating costs, including avoiding the open floor plan concept and removing layers of processes and bureaucracy from the daily work day. The available research has also found that killing the nine-to-five concept and letting people work flexible hours as well as offering more remote work time over the stale work day stuck in a cubicle resulted in happier, motivated employees who churned out higher productivity.

These tactics and tips primarily require making only a few changes to the structure, organization, and culture of your company—versus a large investment of time and money—making them easy to implement and see almost immediate results.

22

MAKE WELLNESS A PILLAR OF CORPORATE CULTURE

Andrew Medal

Beginning a new job or internship can be an exciting and stressful time. Your employee is eager to prove themselves to their colleagues and managers and excited to learn new skills. While it's good that they're focused on their professional goals and responsibilities, it's important to support them outside of the office, too.

I've been a fitness nut all my life. I attribute a lot of my success as an entrepreneur to the dedication

I have made in improving my mind and body every day. With that said, when I started consulting for companies, I quickly became overwhelmed. As business picked up, my health went down along with my energy and motivation. I was making money, but I was more depressed than I had ever been before. It was a hard lesson to learn, but I realized that no amount of money was worth sacrificing my wellness.

But now is a time when health is being made a larger priority. Healthy bodies and minds go hand in hand with happiness and productivity—both highly sought after characteristics in the workplace. Today's companies, ranging from startups to Fortune 500s, are even introducing comprehensive corporate wellness programs to make health a pillar of corporate culture. Colleagues are exercising, juicing and even meditating together in the office.

From the nap rooms in Zappos' Las Vegas campus to the bike-share programs at Facebook, today's organizations are pulling out all the stops to ensure that their employees remain healthy and happy. Speaking to *Forbes* contributor Kevin Harrington in 2015, Dr. Roger Sahoury, a champion of corporate health, claimed that when individuals recognize the efforts their employers are taking in ensuring their health, it encourages them to work harder at their jobs.

Make wellness a priority in your company, and make sure you communicate that to potential hires. Additionally, you want to ensure you have these two healthy foundations as part of your efforts.

Boundaries

A 24/7, always-on lifestyle is just not sustainable. Too often, employees feel the need to work to the point of exhaustion day in and day out. But this attitude actually doesn't help anyone. The term "burnout" was first used in the 1970s and since then has become an increasing problem plaguing American work culture. Over the past few years, burnout rates have become such a problem that millions of Americans feel there is no other solution but to leave their jobs.

According to the Association for Physiological Science, millions in the American workforce elected to resign in 2014 simply over burnout. Burnout is not inevitable, however. Help your team set themselves up for a long and healthy career by making supporting them in their efforts to set boundaries between their work responsibilities and their personal lives.

People need to leave the office at a reasonable hour, set blackout times in which their teams knows they won't be looking at emails (except in emergency scenarios), and make self-care a priority. Don't be afraid to have frank conversations about typical working hours, weekend emailing policies, and even how most employees spend their lunch break. These issues may seem somewhat trivial, but they offer significant insight into what's expected in your company.

Team Bonding

Building strong relationships with the people they work alongside can be the distinguishing factor in how people feel about their jobs and how they approach their work. Spending time cultivating relationships with team members and managers sets everyone up for success. Encourage these types of interactions in your workplace.

In a recent study by the Queen's School of Business and Gallup Organization, employees who felt disengaged reported lower productivity and more errors. Spending time with coworkers outside of meetings and office hours is beneficial to everyone. But strong relationships don't just happen overnight—they have to be nourished.

You might set up an initiative to pair young professionals and/or new hires with mentors or allow such peer-mentoring to take place in group settings. You don't need elaborate weekly outings.

Simple things such as outdoor team lunches and group yoga classes are key signs that your corporate culture values relationships and overall wellbeing.

Maybe your company is currently lagging behind on the wellness initiatives. You can start small and do things every day to foster strong bonds and encourage healthy habits among your teammates, such as eating lunch away from your desk, going for daily walks, organizing after-work meetups, or setting up daily meditation challenges for your entire team.

It's up to you to make wellness an important part of your work culture.

ENTREPRENEUR VOICES SPOTLIGHT: INTERVIEW WITH TODD GRAVES

Founder, CEO, Fry Cook & Cashier of Raising Cane's

Scale Your Culture Without Losing Your Soul

In Baton Rouge, Louisiana, there are a few cultural institutions that are so ingrained that they become a part of everyday life and the identity of the city. LSU football. Community Coffee. The legacy of Huey P. Long. Perhaps the most recent addition is Raising Cane's.

What, you might ask, is a quick-service chicken finger restaurant doing in a book on company culture for entrepreneurs? The first part of the answer is that "founder, CEO, fry cook, and cashier" Todd Graves is the embodiment of the entrepreneurial spirit. He never took a business class in college, yet he had a dream about opening a chicken finger restaurant. He and his original partner wrote a business plan as a college assignment. The professor gave it the worst grade in the class and told them it would never work. He took his business plan to the banks, and was told it would never work. He decided to bootstrap his dream by working in refineries and then literally risking his life as a commercial fisherman in Alaska à la *Deadliest Catch*. He came home, opened up Raising Cane's (after his dog, whose name is a sweet, sugarcane twist on the phrase "raising Cain"), and is now a multimillionaire.

But the second and more important answer to the question of what do chicken fingers have to do with company culture is actually another question: despite its phenomenal growth, despite having hundreds of locations across dozens of states and a number overseas, despite having thousands of employees, despite having major operations centers in both Baton Rouge and Dallas, despite being the first employer most of its millennial workforce has ever had . . . how has Raising Cane's been able to keep its unique, upbeat culture consistent throughout the world and still be independently ranked in 2017:

- in the top 50 places to work in the U.S. (Glassdoor), appearing on the same list as Facebook, Boston Consulting Group, McKinsey, Apple, and SpaceX—an amazing accolade for any company and that much more for a drive-through restaurant staffed

- as number one in "drive thru speed of service and accuracy" (QSR magazine)—a much-appreciated near miracle if you've ever gone through a drive-through with a picky child

- as number one in "customer intent to return" (Techonomoic)—the holy grail of quick-service restaurants

- as number one in "supports the local community" (Techonomic)—something nearly every company pays lip service to but rarely makes a true priority

- having the highest average gross revenues per restaurant in the industry, second only to Chik-fil-A (Restaurant News)

- . . . and the fastest growing chain in the U.S. (Restaurant News)?

What is this magic formula of Raising Cane's that creates a scalable culture where people love to work, where customers love to return, and that competitors love to hate?

Entrepreneur: Well, Todd, what's the secret?

Graves: Look, it's not rocket science. I fry chicken for a living. That's probably the easiest part of our business.

The hardest part is just staying focused. Everything we do, every decision we make, and everybody's job ties back to the restaurants. Last week we made a three-million-dollar decision to purchase better headsets. Our crews told us they had trouble hearing with the old ones; we listened.

We don't have corporate offices—we have "restaurant support offices." Throughout the company, everybody wears the same Raising Cane's uniforms. Everyone's title is their position plus "fry cook and cashier." No matter who you are, every new hire goes through the same restaurant training. Our restaurants and the people in them are at the center of everything we do.

Entrepreneur: Wait. Everyone goes through restaurant training? As in, everyone everyone?

Graves: Every person who works for Raising Cane's has been a fry cook and a cashier, from our vice president of real estate to my co-CEO. And once a year, we do a total cultural immersion where we take the newly hired leaders of the company and all work a late night together at the original Cane's, and then do another two to three days working in locations around Baton Rouge and revisiting Raising Cane's roots.

When we interview people and tell them that, some of them say, "Great!" Some people say, "Really?"

If you don't like the idea of being hired for marketing and then starting out frying chicken, we understand, but that probably means you won't like it here. And if you don't like it here, that probably means you won't be successful here. That probably means Raising Cane's isn't the best place for you.

We've even had to let people go when we saw that they weren't a good cultural fit. If you have a transactional, short-term perspective, that's fine. The corporate recruiter we work with told me that that's what many of her clients are looking for: someone for a three- to five-year position. But that's not what we're looking for here.

Entrepreneur: So keeping the focus on the restaurants is one piece of the puzzle. Hiring the right corporate employees is another.

Graves: Not just at our restaurant support offices: we want to hire the right people at every level. Each restaurant manager is like the CEO of their restaurant. When we don't have the right leader in place, we can see a drop in revenue as large as 30 percent. The restaurant manager is the most critical hire we make.

But we also want to hire the right crew members at each location. We have an enormous pool of potential hires. As part of the application process, we have people take a personality assessment, which we compare to the tests from some of our best crew members. It helps us immediately spot some of the obvious stuff that wouldn't make for the right fit in the applicant pool.

We want to work hard and have fun. We want our crew members to enjoy serving people. You know those people at a party who are always making sure everyone has something to drink and that everyone's having a good time? Those are the kind of people we want working with us.

We've even had to let some of our franchise partners go. They were great people, but they weren't able to have the crew members in their restaurants emulate their behavior.

Entrepreneur: Hold on: you fired a franchisee? Someone who paid to franchise a Raising Cane's?

Graves: Yeah. I hated to do it. That's why we're more careful now. It's hard to find franchise partners who completely buy in to the "fry cook and cashier" mentality. That's why about 75 percent of our restaurants are company-owned and only 25 percent are franchised, whereas, in our industry it's usually the other way around.

Take our franchise partner in Kuwait, Mohammed Alshaya. He genuinely cares about his people. When I went to talk to him about his interest in franchising Cane's, I flew into Kuwait City a few days early to visit some of the other franchises in the Alshaya group. The people were friendly and outgoing, the stores were nice and clean, and the food and service were excellent. That's what we're looking for in a franchise partner.

Entrepreneur: So, your focus on culture goes beyond just the people who work for you. You want the people who work with you to be a culture fit as well.

Graves: You know, they don't necessarily have to have the same culture we do, but they do need to be value-aligned. We want to work with people who want to deliver great products and services and focus on customer service.

On the East Coast, we buy our chicken from Purdue Farms. On the West Coast, it's Ron Foster. I know our vendors and their companies. I know the way our cup manufacturer and our box supplier do business. When you're manufacturing at scale, something's going to get screwed up, no matter how great your processes are. When it does happen, how do they respond? Do they take care of us and hotshot the corrected cups or relabeled boxes or extra chicken?

Entrepreneur Voices Spotlight: Interview with Todd Graves

We have an operators' meeting in February where I give a state of the company address and we generally have a great time together. We'll even invite our top suppliers. Over those two or three days, I'll take 500 people on tours of Cane's 1—"the mothership," we call it—and let them get a taste of how we do business. We want to be more than just a customer to them, and we want them to be more than just a supplier to us. We are true partners.

Entrepreneur: Todd, what fascinates me about Raising Cane's is that you kept this great vibe and workplace culture and somehow scaled to a national and now international scale. When and where did you make the leap from a local fast-food restaurant with locations in Baton Rouge to a national company?

Graves: We had grown to eight restaurants in Baton Rouge. I just ran around training everybody and working in all the locations. For a hands-on entrepreneur, it's a really hard leap to go to a professionally-managed company and keep that entrepreneurial spirit.

We opened our ninth restaurant in Lafayette. It was just 45 minutes down the road, so it was close enough that I could jump in the car and be there, but far enough way that I couldn't be there constantly. It forced us to create a

Raising Cane's prototype—not just on interior design but for all our systems, like human resources and operations. We had some really great vendor partners who showed us how to create a corporate setup. One of the things they asked me was, "What's your culture?"

Well, I'd never taken a business class in college. I had no idea what they meant.

They said, "How do you treat each other? What does it feel like to work at Raising Cane's?"

I knew how I wanted it to feel, but we decided to ask our crew members: What's it like to work here?

Many of them described it as "cool." Okay, but cool *how*?

"We treat each other right." "You're positive—you find the good things." "We have a good time." "We get to listen to music in the kitchen."

That's what made Raising Cane's what it really is: that cool vibe. When we scaled, we didn't want to lose that. We wanted our crew members—and these were all Millennial college students at the time—to keep that feeling.

We've never had a script. We want our crew members to welcome the customer, deliver the perfect box, and thank them for their business, but however they want to do that is up to them.

If we told our cashiers, "Here's what you're going to say when someone walks in the door," we'd lose our coolness in two seconds. We let our crew members own their job and have as much autonomy as they can. As long as it aligns with our values and doesn't violate any of our non-negotiables, we're cool with it.

We want to be authentic. When we advertise on a billboard, we feature a local manager on it. When we film a commercial, we use actual crew members. When we record a radio commercial, that's my dog barking.

Entrepreneur: It sounds like there's not any one magic bullet. It's all these things working together that lets you scale your culture—quite profitably, I might add.

Graves: Like I said, this isn't rocket science. Our culture evolved from a deep appreciation for our crew members, our customers, and our communities. We love our people, and we love our chicken.

Entrepreneur: Any chance I can get the recipe for Cane's secret sauce from you?

Graves: Sure! First, you . . .

end recording

PART III
TOOLS AND TACTICS—REFLECTIONS

Most business owners and managers probably feel more comfortable with this section than the others. Entrepreneurs are problem solvers by their very nature. When something's not working well, they want to step in, come up with an innovative solution, and spearhead its implementation.

Having concrete, tangible, step-by-step ways to tackle the "culture thing" lets company leaders feel like they have a project. "Let's create our own People Analyzer." "Let's get everyone set up on TINYPulse." "Let's schedule a once-a-month game night."

Turning culture into a task list with nice boxes to check off—well, that'd be nice, wouldn't it? But this book's four sections are arranged in somewhat chronological order: before you start using these tools and tactics to support your efforts to build a better culture, you should first gain clarity about the culture you want in the first place (section I) and then figure out how to personally lead your people towards that vision (section II). Only then does it make sense to use tools and tactics to support you in that journey.

Otherwise, these are solutions in search of a problem.

Bill Gates once said,

> *The first rule of any technology used in a business is that automation applied to an efficient operation will magnify the efficiency. The second is that automation applied to an inefficient operation will magnify the inefficiency.*

The spirit of that quote is essentially what we're saying right here.

Refer back to Steffen Maier's article on Google and the employee survey. When employees don't believe in the company in the first place, the tools used to help improve culture are ineffective. You need a certain amount of trust and healthy culture established before applying particular tools.

But having clarity and leadership *plus* tools and tactics is a recipe for success.

DYSFUNCTION

n *The 100 Best Business Books of All Time*, the authors wrote, "The number one reason people buy business books is to find solutions to problems."

You're holding this business book in your hands. You probably bought it because you're looking for a solution to a problem. This book was written for entrepreneurs and is about company culture. *Ipso facto*, your company has a problem with its culture.

Perhaps you wouldn't quite characterize it as dysfunctional, as this section is named, but the fact remains that you're likely reading this because the environment at your business is—sub-optimal, shall we say? As such, it makes sense that the section that speaks most directly to your reason for buying the book should have more space devoted to it than the other three.

The good news is that we want to help you turn things around. As noted earlier, culture is often pushed to the side until it becomes a problem. If you don't like how things look in your company, you're experiencing the same feeling many entrepreneurs do. Having a less-than-ideal culture is normal—regrettable, but normal.

Fortunately, in keeping with the spirit of earlier sections, most of the advice in this one is easy to implement. Not one of the authors suggests hiring an outside consultancy or bringing in mediators. While those professionals have their place, "change has to come from within." Yes, it's a cliché, but that's because it's one of those fundamental truths that we seem to constantly circle back to.

In perhaps one of the most poignant pieces in this compilation, you're going to read about the CEO of a tech company who admits that his company had a fundamentally flawed culture—and then the steps the executive team took to turn it around. Their culture makeover didn't take money or even a substantial investment of time; it took courage.

Spoiler alert: his story has a happy ending.

23

HOW A CEO CAN FIX CORPORATE CULTURE

Shellye Archambeau

When corporate culture makes the news, it's usually for all the wrong reasons. United Airlines has become almost infamous for its treatment of passengers from the viral hit "United Breaks Guitars" to the viral video of the doctor being dragged down the aisle.

But for every company whose culture results in these types of newsworthy stories, there is a Southwest Airlines, famous for its employees-first mantra and spirit of inclusiveness that inspire teams to go the extra mile for customers. There is a Quicken Loans, whose "isms" or cultural values—like "simplicity is genius" and "yes before no"—have led the company to become one of the fastest growing online mortgage lenders, not to mention one of *Fortune* magazine's top ten best companies to work for.

We could examine what's wrong with United's culture (or any of dozens of companies famous for their awful employee engagement practices). But a good company culture isn't just about avoiding doing the wrong things; it's also about doing the right things.

In successful companies, culture goes beyond free yoga classes, gourmet meals, and other perks. It's about creating a work environment based on shared values and principles—ideals so deeply embedded in the organization's DNA that they become intrinsic to daily decisions. It is about building a business where people can collectively thrive and grow. It's about an environment where people are driven to do good work—better work— that translates into higher customer satisfaction and better performance. Culture is the glue that binds a company together. As with most things in a business, it starts at the top.

What can a CEO do to improve corporate culture?

Listen More, Talk Less

When you're busy running a company, it's easy to miss what's happening on the frontlines. Would employees at Wells Fargo have created those millions of fake bank and credit card accounts if executives had actually listened to their employees, and understood the pressures that they were under to meet sales targets? Employees live the organization's culture every day, and if something is not quite right, they are the first ones to know—which is why it so important to tune in to what they are saying.

Website design startup Squarespace keeps its finger on the pulse of the organization by maintaining a flat, open culture where there are minimal levels of management between staff and executives. This gives employees the confidence to voice their opinions freely.

Encouraging open dialog is important. At MetricStream, I keep a stuffed elephant in my office. It is meant as a reminder that I encourage team members to "put the elephants on the table." You could conduct surveys to collect employee feedback, talk to your staff face-to-face, or establish hotlines where people can report grievances and concerns without fear of being targeted.

As you listen, pay attention to the sub-text and non-verbal cues. Employees might be telling you one thing, but their expressions and gestures might be signifying the opposite. Are they afraid to speak the truth? If so, what does that say about your culture? Similarly, when sending out surveys, take note of how many people respond or how many questions they skipped. At team meetings, observe how people interact. Do they look engaged? Do they ask questions? These signals provide important insights into your organization's culture and its alignment with corporate values.

Reward employees for speaking up and raising issues. Invite them to challenge your thoughts and bring diverse ideas and opinions to the table. When employees feel that they are being heard and know their concerns are noted, they will be more engaged, productive, and innovative.

Make Collaboration the Core of Your Culture

At the 2016 Rio Olympics, the Japanese 4x100 meters relay team pulled off an unexpected victory when it defeated North American sprinting legends to win the silver. None of the four Japanese men by themselves were as fast as America's Justin Gatlin or Canada's Andre De Grasse. However, what they lacked in speed, they made up for in teamwork and seamless baton changes that ultimately gave them the winning edge.

Noted leadership expert Ken Blanchard once said, "None of us is as smart as all of us." Effective leaders understand this concept. They know that the best corporate cultures are created when people work as one unit towards common goals and values—when individual contributions come together to drive collective achievements.

However, fostering a spirit of collaboration in today's scattered, global organizations can be challenging. Many leaders limit collaboration to specific projects rather than viewing it as the bedrock of a successful organization. There are others who understand that one of the most basic human needs is to belong; when employees feel they're a valued member of a team that collaborates towards a meaningful purpose, they tend to be more innovative, high-performing, and satisfied.

Collaboration doesn't happen by accident, though. It takes a strong, sustained strategy and roadmap. Begin by helping employees realize the importance of collaboration--not only in achieving the organization's objectives--but also in fulfilling their own unique potential. Create a work environment of trust and respect where employees are free to express themselves. Invite them to work across silos with other teams and functions. Establish metrics that can measure and improve the level of collaboration.

Embrace the idea that "the whole is greater than the sum of its parts."

Encourage Risk-Taking

As someone who has spent much of her life taking risks, both as an individual and as the CEO of a company, I've learned that the most successful businesses are those unafraid to take chances. YouTube CEO Susan Wojcicki put it best when she said, "Life doesn't always present you with the perfect opportunity at the perfect time . . . . Opportunities—the good ones—they're messy and confusing and hard to recognize. They're risky. They challenge you."

The only way to realize these opportunities is to establish a culture of risk-taking where employees across the organization are empowered to experiment and challenge the status quo. At MetricStream, one of our biggest innovations yet—the M7 GRC platform and apps—is the cumulative result of teams across the organization pushing the boundaries of technology to boldly go where few, if any, companies have gone before.

A strong culture of risk-taking is particularly important in a world that is constantly changing. If you want to innovate, transform, and disrupt, your employees have to take those leaps of faith. It starts with walking the talk: when employees see their leaders taking smart risks, they will follow suit.

You also need informed decision-making. Employees have to understand the risks they're taking. Encourage them to spend time measuring and analyzing the possible risks of their ideas so that they are prepared for the outcomes. Establish milestones, check-posts, and controls to ensure the risks don't spin out of control. Let employees know it's ok if things don't always work out.

When Google's much hyped Wave failed, then-CEO Eric Schmidt told reporters, "Remember, we celebrate our failures. This is a company where it's absolutely ok to try something that's very hard, have it not be successful, and take the learning from that."

Culture is not something that just happens. Like anything worthwhile, it takes time, effort, and commitment. Take a leaf out of Asana's book. The tech company treats culture as a product that, like any app or software, requires careful design, testing, and debugging in endless iterations. Representatives from across the company meet regularly to take stock of corporate values and identify new ways to embed them. They also collect user feedback about what's working well and what is not. Unsurprisingly, the company was recently named among *Entrepreneur*'s best company cultures of 2017.

At the end of the day, companies like Asana know that culture is not just a "nice-to-have." It is as important as the product or service you're selling because when you have a robust, cohesive culture, you have happy employees. And when you have happy employees, you have higher productivity, happier customers, and stronger profits.

FIXING UBER'S MISTAKES

Nina Zipkin

During a Tuesday meeting to discuss an overhaul of Uber's company culture, former board member David Bonderman proved exactly why such conversations needed to happen in the first place.

At the start of the all-hands meeting, Arianna Huffington, who was the first woman to join the company's board last year, announced the addition of Nestlé executive Wan Ling Martello to the board, increasing the representation of women on the board from 14 to 25 percent.

"There's a lot of data that shows when there's one woman on the board, it's much more likely that there will be a second woman on the board," Huffington noted.

That's when Bonderman interrupted.

"Actually, what it shows is it's much likely to be more talking."

In the recording obtained by *Yahoo Finance*, you can hear Huffington respond at first with awkward laughter, and then reply, "Oh. Come on, David. Don't worry, David will have a lot more talking to do as well."

That is not to be the case, as Bonderman resigned shortly after the meeting, which, it bears repeating, was convened to talk about recommendations to change Uber's culture after allegations of systemic discrimination and sexual harassment.

Bonderman, the 74-year-old founding partner of investment firm TPG Capital, apologized for the "disrespectful" comment via an internal memo to Uber employees and issued this statement about his departure:

> *I do not want my comments to create distraction as Uber works to build a culture of which we can be proud. I need to hold myself to the same standards that we're asking Uber to adopt. Therefore, I have*

decided to resign from Uber's board of directors, effective tomorrow morning.

Earlier, CEO Travis Kalanick also announced that he would be taking a leave of absence, as he shared in an email to the company, in order to:

. . . take some time off of the day-to-day to grieve my mother, whom I buried on Friday, to reflect, to work on myself, and to focus on building out a world-class leadership team. The ultimate responsibility, for where we've gotten and how we've gotten here, rests on my shoulders. There is of course much to be proud of but there is much to improve. For Uber 2.0 to succeed, there is nothing more important than dedicating my time to building out the leadership team. But if we are going to work on Uber 2.0, I also need to work on Travis 2.0 to become the leader that this company needs and that you deserve.

So, what exactly is Uber 2.0 going to look like?

Over the past few months, former attorney general Eric Holder and Tammy Albarrán, partners at law firm Covington & Burling, were tasked with investigating the allegations made by former engineer Susan Fowler and others.

They interviewed more than 200 Uber employees and provided a set of recommendations pertaining to how the company should address discrimination, harassment, and retaliation and how it could "ensure that its commitment to a diverse and inclusive workplace was reflected not only in the company's policies but made real in the experiences of each of Uber's employees."

The recommendations include:

- Providing more support for the human resources department and establishing clear protocols to track complaints
- Mandatory training for senior executives, HR staffers, managers, and people in the position to interview prospective employees, particularly around the topics of promoting inclusion and combatting unconscious bias
- In terms of recruiting and developing talent, implementing a blind resume review and increased transparency when it comes to performance reviews and promotions
- The prohibition of romantic or intimate relationships between supervisor/subordinates and the consumption of alcohol during work hours, at after work events, and at company-sponsored events
- An update of discrimination and harassment policies including instituting a zero-tolerance policy for violators of those rules—no matter

what position they hold in the company—
and explicit protection against harassment
from not only other employees but third-
parties the company deals with from clients
to vendors

A lot of these seem quite standard. But when you
look at former engineer Susan Fowler's blog post
and Kalanick's 2013 Miami letter side by side, the
necessity for Holder and Albarrán to explicitly state
things such as the importance of "de-emphasizing
alcohol as a component of work events" or that
policies should be applied consistently across the
company with no special treatment afforded to any
one employee is pretty glaring.

One passage in particular about Uber's 14
cultural values speaks volumes about where Uber
ran aground. Holder and Albarrán recommended
that the company communicate with its employees
to reassess and develop a core list of values that are
accessible and easy to understand.

The recommendation reads:

*Eliminate those values which have been identified
as redundant or as having been used to justify poor
behavior, including Let Builders Build, Always
Be Hustlin', Meritocracy and Toe-Stepping, and
Principled Confrontation; and encourage senior*

*leaders to exhibit the values on a daily basis and
to model a more collaborative and inclusive Uber
culture. Leaders who embody these values should
be part of the process of redefining Uber's values
and should be role models for other leaders within
the company.*

Uber has long had a reputation for aggressive
tactics in its dealings with regulators and competitors.
It was seen, for better or worse, as one of the key
drivers of its rapid growth. But clearly, as Uber's
experience shows us, growth and success are not one
in the same.

In an interview with *Vanity Fair* in 2014, Kara
Swisher asked Kalanick about the nature of the
interactions with the leaders of the cities his business
was disrupting, some of whom he described as
"really awesome, but most are uninspired." He
said:

*If you don't agree with the core principles, which
are the premise of that compromise, then you have
to have what I call principled confrontation. And
so that is the thing that we do that I think can rub
some people the wrong way.*

If you're beginning with the premise that
compromise doesn't work for you and every
interaction is a war of attrition, you can let people

build all they want. But then what, exactly, are you working toward?

If you're always hustlin'—though if they do keep that one, I would urge them to restore the "g" to its rightful place—you don't stop to think about where the pitfalls may be or whether you might be in the wrong. Uber's experience shows us that kind of approach is a recipe for collapsing under the weight of your own hubris.

In Uber's San Francisco headquarters, up until this week, the office's main conference room was called aptly, the War Room. *Bloomberg* reported that along with the multitude of changes recommended by Covington & Burling, the room is now going to be called the Peace Room. It's a bit on nose, but you can appreciate the thought, as long as it's not just lip service.

Uber's culture is not going to change overnight, but now the company seems to have the self-awareness and tools in place to build an environment where values aren't used, as per Holder and Albarrán's description, to "justify poor behavior."

So, what can we learn from Uber's newfound emphasis on internal, rather than external growth? Company culture isn't about perks or empty aphorisms that look good on a T-shirt. Simply, people want to be heard, they want their work to be valued, and they want to be treated with respect.

When you build your company culture, start there.

25

WHEN YOUR COMPANY HAS A "BEST BUTT" AWARD

Ray Hennessey

It seems like on the first day of a new job, covering sexual harassment is pretty standard. Often, such training is accompanied by videos that show what isn't acceptable in a professional setting. For instance, telling a coworker they have a nice butt isn't a good idea.

That's why a controversy at an Indiana restaurant chain is such a head-scratcher. At least one manager at Scotty's Brewhouse in Indianapolis was fired as a result of a team-building event gone wrong. Several employees received trophies akin to "best bartender" or "best server," presumably as some kind of reward for good service.

But one employee got a trophy that was entirely unwelcome: "best butt." Not only that, but after receiving the trophy, she was then told to turn around in front of everyone so people could take pictures of the asset that earned her the award.

The server, not identified by the local media, was, unsurprisingly, not amused. In fact, she felt humiliated.

"I feel like I'm more than just a butt," the woman told a local television station. "I feel like I'm smart. I'm going to school."

In fact, she deserved a trophy for nothing short of work ethic, it seems. "I have two jobs so I can make money and continue to go to school, and then get my degree and not work two jobs anymore."

The corporate bosses at Scotty's meted out an ass-whooping for the offense. In a statement, company owner Scott Wise said he was "completely unaware" of the awards, nor did he or anyone else in senior management "condone or sponsor this event."

"As a result," Wise said, "we took immediate action that included terminating management, and

I have instructed our teams to immediately do additional sexual harassment training companywide, beyond the initial training process new managers go through already when they are hired."

From a communications standpoint, that touches on the Holy Trinity of messaging companies want to make in a crisis like this: "It was an isolated incident, we handled it swiftly, and we're working to make sure it never happens again."

But there's also something hollow about the response. Sexual harassment policies, like all corporate efforts to root out bad behavior and discrimination, can be filled with gray areas. All hiring, for instance, involves some kind of discrimination. Many managers have spent a good amount of time wondering whether a colleague's compliment over a dress runs afoul of unwelcome-communications policies and needs a disciplinary response.

In this instance, though, there isn't a gray area. Talking about someone's butt to them is an event worthy of termination at most places, for obvious reasons: it objectifies someone in a sexually aggressive away, which runs a high risk of being unwelcome by the receiver. That's first-day training material: no touching, no whistling, no hooting.

Having an *engraved* trophy takes this to a whole other level.

And that's where an isolated firing and retraining might not do the trick Scotty's management needs. Many employees test company policies, but only enterprises with permissive cultures allow some to blow past boundaries in the way that happened with the "best butt" trophy. It's probably not surprising that this happened in a bar environment, which is more laid back than a cubicle-farm office. A neon Bud sign is a modern *sub rosa*, a signal that much of what happens in the confine of the bar is meant to stay there--or at least to never be mentioned (or remembered) again. Many employees at bars and restaurants know and accept this. The banter that goes on in kitchens or behind bar with staff would make a Teamster blush and cause blood-pressure spikes in the average HR representative.

But that's no license to humiliate or take away human dignity from someone, and that's what happened at Scotty's. Beyond simply a rogue employee or two, Scotty's corporate culture bears some responsibility and needs an assessment. After all, it was Scotty's overall culture that, presumably, allowed people to be hired and promoted to the point where a "best butt" trophy didn't command a second thought. At the very least, it's a cultural indictment that a single management team at one restaurant could have an event like this without anyone in the corporate suites knowing about it or approving of it beforehand. Yes, all companies have bad employees and subpar managers, but bad culture often allows these people to go unchecked. That's the blame of leadership--not the bad actors in question.

Here's the good news. Scotty's seems like a great business. It's been around 20 years, has about a dozen restaurants, and looks to be welcoming and inventive with its food. (I'm particularly intrigued by something called a Chupacabra burger.) This isn't some roadside trucker tavern that can't get out of its own way. It seems to have bright marketing minds, committed leadership, and knows a crisis when it sees one. A cultural audit is at least easy to begin, even if the findings are troubling.

And there's better news: Scotty's can use this to try to hire more people who work their tails off, support themselves, pay for their education and contribute to a positive workplace culture.

That would be a very nice end.

26

WHEN REBEL.COM NEEDED A CULTURE MAKEOVER

Rob Villeneuve

L ess than two years ago, the corporate culture at my web-hosting company, Rebel.com, needed serious attention. We could feel it in the air. Besides that, we had a one-star rating on Glassdoor to prove it. But, oh, have things changed.

Today, we love the culture we have, though it took a lot of hard work to get it to where it is. Launching a new brand wasn't the only catalyst we had for raising our score to a 4.4. We had to work on our core identity.

When we first learned about our low employee satisfaction score, we knew we had to act. It's impossible to be customer-centric if you're not employee-centric, and our employees were clearly frustrated with the company. In our search for a better culture, we discovered the five major insights that eventually helped turn our company around.

1. Recognize the Disengaged

Disengaged employees are the ones who encourage mutinies, pass on vicious gossip, and hurt brand and client relationships along the way. These employees have 37 percent higher absenteeism, 49 percent more work-related accidents, and 60 percent more errors in their work.

They do just enough to meet expectations—no more and no less. They don't build energy or have a team mentality. Allowing disengaged employees to have influence at your company can multiply the amount of overall mediocre work, negativity, and stress.

We started turning our culture around by giving disengaged employees our attention. We took the time to listen, share insights, and set up tools that would reduce their frustration. Many of those disengaged employees quickly became positive influencers. In a culture of listening, the truly disengaged are an exception, not the rule. If an employee doesn't want to change their tune after being heard, you may need to part ways with them.

As we hired new employees, we incorporated engagement strategies right into our system of onboarding, which in turn helped integrate those new hires into our culture from day one.

2. Listen. Really Listen.

Engaged employees should also know they're being listened to. Research shows employees are 100 percent more likely to be actively disengaged when they're ignored. It takes a great deal of bravery for managers to open themselves to possible criticism, but that openness is part of what makes a great leader.

This doesn't just mean asking if there are any questions or concerns at the end of a meeting. Not everyone feels comfortable airing grievances in public. That's why anonymous feedback and collaborative tools, such as TINYpulse and SpeakUp, should be used for better communication.

Although the results aren't always flattering, the candid feedback is necessary, so long as employees are encouraged to provide both problems *and* solutions.

3. Don't Punish Criticism

Instead of trying to crush the criticism, we decided to embrace it to learn more about each issue to find solutions. Anonymous feedback tools ensure that employees don't fear reprisal for providing honest feedback. If there's anything an employee doesn't feel comfortable saying in a one-on-one meeting, they should always feel comfortable saying it through an anonymous platform.

To alleviate fears, we held companywide meetings to communicate with our team that negative feedback would not be punished. We gave examples of how to address concerns and celebrated the courage it took to contribute with honest feedback—even the negative variety. Between the meetings and forms, we gathered all the open feedback we needed to take action and turn things around.

4. Never Leave Questions or Ideas Unaddressed

Letting feedback sit, untouched, was the same as telling our employees we didn't care. Feedback is useless without action, whether that means simply explaining why a process is in place or reviewing the company's systematic problems and brainstorming ways to improve them.

To gain trust, my management team and I realized we had to take action. We started with simple changes and made the time to address the harder pieces. We updated the staff on our progress regularly and publicly held ourselves accountable. Regular one-on-one meetings help both employees and leaders understand one other's perspectives and open communication to address any problems. Today, we operate in a model of continual improvements—the work is never done.

5. Own Up to Your Mistakes

When employees are brave enough to point out mistakes, leadership needs to be strong enough to own up to them. Part of transparency involves admitting mistakes and soliciting solutions to involve employees in the results. This will unite you and your employees toward a common problem and let them know you're human.

Recently, we mistakenly failed to communicate a new policy early to employees. This made employees upset, so they worked together to communicate feedback to management. Within 48 hours, the problem was identified, discussed, and resolved because both sides were willing to collaborate.

Like any change initiative, it's necessary to quantify improvement. Team surveys where managers and employees rate themselves and each other every three to six months are easy ways to accomplish that. This allows progress to be tracked over time and improvement to be shown in key areas.

For Rebel.com, the quantification came from our improved Glassdoor score and survey results. We are now addicted to continuously improving our culture because it creates a happy place to work. Doing so has improved our business performance in ways we'd never imagined.

It was painful to discover our culture was not where we wanted it to be, but listening was an important lesson to learn. Company culture is an iterative process: you listen to feedback, create a solution, and measure results. If you've done well, that's great. If not, keep trying.

Is your company struggling with culture and engagement? Re-evaluating your communication could be the difference between an authentic culture you're proud of and a company without employees.

THE EASY WAY TO IMPROVE EMPLOYEE ENGAGEMENT

Matthew Baker

Employers take note: you're not holding the attention or interest of your employees. Think you're an exception to the rule? Think again. Seventy percent of American employees report being disengaged at work and three out of four are currently looking for a new job or are open to new opportunities.

While there is something to be said for options and hedging the risk of potential layoffs, this means more than half of your workforce is not passionate about what they're doing or committed to your organization.

Disengaged employees are doing a huge disservice to every aspect of your business. Research suggests they negatively affect everything from team morale to productivity to your bottom line.

While this paints a dreary picture, the good news is companies can take steps toward boosting employee engagement. Traditional efforts include internal mobility programs, employee wellness initiatives, and appropriately rewarding behavior. But these can be a drain on resources and cost a lot of money. So, what's the cost-effective secret to improving employee engagement?

Building and maintaining a values-based culture.

A Culture Rooted in Values

Workplace culture is often misunderstood, and many measure it by the number of nap rooms and ping-pong tables. However, at its core, a successful culture is a system of shared beliefs and behaviors members of the workplace use to interact with one another.

Values capture what an organization believes is most important to the way it operates, such as teamwork, creativity, or diversity. Values are open to interpretation and, above all, dogmatic. A values-based culture exists when employees associate meaning to their behaviors based on specific company values.

Not sure if you have a values-based culture? Ask a few of your employees about a challenging decision they faced and which beliefs helped them reach a decision. Did they behave according to their own personal values? Financial goals? Emotional attachment? Or was the decision attributed to your company's values?

Values Set Boundaries and Provide Flexibility

A values-based culture relies on employee autonomy and empowerment to function. An individual is much more likely to drive better results when they feel ownership over their work. Values provide clear boundaries, but the space inside the boundaries is for exploration and innovation, allowing employees more freedom to shape the work they're doing.

The exercise of making decisions within a values-based culture fosters engagement. Conversely, making decisions solely based on a set of workflows, processes, and calculations requires intelligence and attention to detail. But frankly, it's boring and doesn't adequately capture and sustain the attention and interest of employees.

Large and small companies can benefit from a values-based culture. Moreover, the values from one organization to the next can be completely different.

A Look at Values-Based Cultures

McKinsey & Company, a Top 25 Places to Work, is a management consulting firm with more than 10,000 employees across 100 offices globally. The firm has three governing values:

- Adhere to the highest professional standards
- Improve our clients' performance significantly
- Create an unrivaled environment for exceptional people

One of the ways McKinsey & Company reinforces its values-based culture is an annual event called "Values Day." On this day, each office sets aside time to discuss what the values mean, including role-playing scenarios where the values are tested in challenging situations.

Another company that practices values-based culture is FreshBooks, a software company with 250 employees based in Toronto, Canada. The company has nine core values: passion, ownership, respect, change, honesty, fun, empathy, strive, and trust.

To bring these values to life, FreshBooks hosts an annual company retreat in honor of the values called

PORCHFEST (the acronym is based on the first letter of each value) and offers an ongoing program called "Values Cards" encouraging employees to nominate each other for a gift card when their behavior epitomizes one of the values. One card, for example, read, "Samantha recently exhibited the value of Change by embracing a last-minute detour in the launch calendar that resulted in more work for her."

Other examples aren't hard to come by. Union Square Hospitality Group, chosen as one of the original Small Giants, lives by four "Family Values": excellence, hospitality, entrepreneurial spirit, and integrity. Southwest Airlines, with a full-time culture director and more than 50,000 employees, has four company values: warrior spirit, servant's heart, fun-LUVing attitude, and work the Southwest way.

In each of these examples, the values are drastically different. Yet, if values are instilled in the culture, they capture the essence of a company's way of living and represent the most effective way to engage employees.

More companies should take time to live and breathe company values. When values are written down and discussed openly and consistently, all employees can better engage in the company's future.

28

PUBLICITY STUNTS ≠ GOOD CULTURE

Ray Hennessey

Startup Boxed Wholesale decided to offer an innovative employee benefit: paying for a wedding for its employees, up to $20,000. Boxed CEO Chieh Huang told Quartz he considered good, old-fashioned pay raises but decided to invest in benefits instead. (A Boxed spokesperson later stressed that raises still happen based on performance reviews.)

The wedding payment plan yielded a slew of positive press, and Boxed Wholesale, like Zappos, is quickly becoming one of those companies that pundits and journalists point to when they want to show the pinnacle of great corporate culture.

In reality, though, Boxed is one of those companies that misses the point of what good culture is, also like Zappos. In fact, Boxed Wholesale's latest perk can just as easily be viewed as a discriminatory and shallow publicity stunt that masks what could later be deeper problems in the organization—again, like Zappos.

Having a great company culture takes hard work. While it requires intention on the part of business leaders to create a solid culture, it also takes acceptance and adoption on the part of the rank and file. That's why perks are so often a red herring: A company with ice cream socials and all-expenses-paid Grubhub accounts can have lousy culture. When *Entrepreneur* and CultureIQ set out to rank the companies with the best company culture, we evaluated ten different areas, including collaboration, communication, and values. "Perks and benefits" wasn't a criterion.

The trouble with the focus on culture nowadays is it that it too often becomes limiting rather than freeing. At its worst, some culture programs are downright discriminatory, with their focus on "fit"—a code word at startups that usually requires you act and think exactly like the founding team.

A wedding benefit is, by its very nature, exclusionary. It only applies to people getting married. If you're already married, the company isn't going to reimburse you the cost of your celebrant and hall. If you choose to stay single, you don't get a check. While the company says no one has complained yet, this is a benefit that by its nature segregates its employees. Truth is, so did the last big benefit Boxed touted, paying for the college tuition of his employees' children.

Look at it this way: you get extra money from Boxed if you get married and send your kids to college. I'm not one of those who believes that using the phrase "starting a family" is somehow objectionable, nor am I as quick to find offense as many are. But based on the benefits being offered employees, you get a sense of what kind of employee Boxed wants. Better put, if I were a trial lawyer, I could at least make a pretty good case of what kind of employee Boxed is looking for.

What's more, it's a silly benefit to offer. A wedding is indeed expensive. If I were a Boxed employee, the company would probably have to raise a separate venture round just to pay for the three I've had. But while pricey, a wedding isn't a hardship. In announcing the new benefit, Chieh Huang was quoted as saying, "We just felt like once someone is part of the Boxed family, we want to be there for them in their time of need."

Time of need? Yes, sometimes life throws you curveballs—the company says it instituted a benefit because an employee's wedding fund was depleted caring for a sick family member—but a wedding is a simple contract between two people in love. A justice of the peace doesn't cost much. The reasons weddings are so important is that we tend to over-do them: china patterns, flowers, passé hors d'oeuvres, and a five-tier cake. There's an industry behind weddings that wraps itself in the cloak of love and good feelings but really should be wearing a ski mask as it relieves you of your wallet.

A wedding is in no way a "time of need." Watching a loved one struggle through cancer, having a sick child, fighting a foreclosure—those are times of need. Those are especially tough to handle when, like an employee of one of Boxed's fulfillment facilities, you're only making $14 an hour.

I have no doubt that Chieh Huang legitimately wants to help. So do most CEOs. My experience has been that great CEOs leading companies with great culture often go out of their way to identify needs among their employees and dig deep to help. Sometimes, they use their companies' funds to help, but they often make a personal act of charity. More importantly, they keep it to themselves. That's a requirement of a good leader.

That's also my last objection to Boxed's walk down the aisle of shame: it's so public. Intentions aside, it's hard to fight criticism that Boxed's wedding benefit is just a publicity stunt when you unleash your publicity apparatus in support of it. The company issued a press release and made sure that the press knows what a great company Boxed is to work for. That's actually a bad communications strategy. It's reminiscent of when the CEO of Gravity Payments crowed he was setting a minimum salary of $70,000 for all his employees—an announcement made with network television cameras rolling and major-market newspapers given embargoed releases and interviews. We know how that turned out.

Good company culture goes well beyond perks. Perks, more often than not, mask cultural problems. And just because you think you're "doing good" as a leader doesn't mean you are actually doing something right. In an era when competition is high for the best and brightest employees, strong pay, generous benefits, open lines of communication from the C-suite on down, and a strong mission are what set apart the strongest companies from the pretenders making noise through a steady stream of press releases and stunts.

CUTTHROAT CULTURES DON'T WORK

Travis Bradberry

F ar too many companies believe that a cutthroat, pressure-cooker culture gets results. They think that the harder they crack that whip, the better people will perform.

Cutthroat business culture is so prevalent that it's a cliché in our society, serving as the inspiration for countless TV shows and movies. The sad thing is that people relate to it on the screen because they've seen it firsthand.

But just because everybody seems to be doing it doesn't mean it works; it just makes it easier to stick your head in the sand and ignore the consequences. But make no mistake: the costs associated with treating people poorly are real.

High-pressure, cutthroat organizations spend 50 percent more on healthcare for their employees than organizations with a more positive, supportive environment because 80 percent of workplace accidents are attributed to stress, as are 80 percent of doctor visits.

Cutthroat organizations are *less* productive because they experience significantly lower levels of employee engagement. Organizations with high numbers of disengaged employees have 40 percent lower earnings per share, are 18 percent less productive, and have 50 percent higher turnover.

If you're leading a cutthroat workplace, it's probably negatively affecting your employees' health. If you aren't yet motivated to take action, consider how the following hallmarks of cutthroat environments suck the life out of people.

1. They Overwork People

Nothing burns good employees out quite like overworking them. It's so tempting to work your best people hard that leaders frequently fall into this trap. Overworking good employees often perplexes the worker. It makes them feel as if they're being punished for a great performance.

Overworking employees is also counter-productive. New research from Stanford shows that productivity per hour declines sharply when the workweek exceeds 50 hours, and productivity drops off so much after 55 hours that employers don't get anything out of the extra hours.

2. There's No Empathy

Empathy matters. Do you really see your employees as people and care how they're doing? Or are you only focused on how much work they churn out? More than half of people who leave their jobs do so because of their relationships with their bosses. Smart companies make certain that their managers know how to balance being professional with being human. These are the bosses who empathize with those going through hard times, yet still challenge people. Bosses who fail to really care will always have high turnover rates. It's impossible to work for someone for eight-plus hours a day when you aren't personally involved with them and don't care about anything other than their production yield.

3. There's No Recognition of Good Work

It's easy to underestimate the power of a pat on the back, especially when it comes to top performers who are intrinsically motivated. Everyone likes kudos, none more so than those who work hard and give their all. Leaders need to communicate with their people to find out what makes them feel good. For some, it's a raise, while for others, it may be public recognition. Then, they need to reward them for a job well done. With top performers, this will happen often if you're doing it right.

4. There's No Socializing and No Fun

Strong social connections are an integral part of a healthy workplace. People who have strong connections with their colleagues get sick less often, are less likely to become depressed, learn faster, remember more, and simply do a better job. People don't give their all if they aren't having fun, and fun is a major protector against burnout. The best companies to work for know the importance of letting employees loosen up a little. Google, for example, does just about everything it can to make work fun—free meals, bowling allies, and fitness classes, to name a few. The idea is simple: if work is fun, you'll not only perform better, but you'll stick around for longer hours and an even longer career.

5. Lots of Stupid Rules

Companies need to have rules. That's a given. But they don't have to be shortsighted and lazy attempts at creating order. Whether it's an overzealous attendance policy or taking employees' frequent flier miles, even a couple of such unnecessary rules can drive people crazy. When good employees feel as though big brother is watching, they'll find someplace else to work.

6. No One Helps Anyone

There's a big difference between delegating responsibility and abdicating it. A boss who abdicates responsibility thinks that it's the employee's problem and that they alone are responsible for solving it. However, research shows that managers who support their employees in tasks that they delegate produce better team players who are more willing to help others and are more committed to their jobs.

7. People Can't Pursue Their Passions

Google mandates that employees spend at least 20 percent of their time doing "what they believe will benefit Google most." While these passion projects make major contributions to marquee Google products, such as Gmail and AdSense, their biggest impact is in creating highly engaged Googlers. Talented employees are passionate; providing opportunities for them to pursue their passions improves their productivity and job satisfaction.

Unfortunately, many leaders want people to work within a little box, fearing that productivity will decline if they let people expand their focus and pursue their passions. This fear is unfounded. Studies have shown that people who are able to pursue their passions at work experience "flow, a euphoric state of mind that is five times more productive than the norm.

8. Leaders Don't Listen

When employees feel that their managers are approachable, supportive, and willing to listen, performance improves. That feeling of connection leads to a willingness to experiment and take risks, which in turn, leads to better outcomes. On the other hand, if conversations between managers and employees never extend beyond TPS reports, and any attempts to ask questions or offer suggestions are rebuffed, the work environment is probably cutthroat.

So what should you do if you find yourself leading a cutthroat environment? I can't answer that question for you. What I can do is tell you that the mental, physical, and financial consequences are real.

FIVE SIGNS YOUR COMPANY IS DOOMED

Craig Cincotta

As companies of all shapes and sizes continue to compete for world class talent, culture becomes a very important part of the decision-making process. People want a place where they can do their best and feel like their contributions are meaningful and their roles valued.

During my career, I have worked in a big company setting at Microsoft, and for the last two years I have done the startup thing at Porch. In both instances I have been fortunate to work with people who appreciate the importance of culture. But that isn't always the case. There are companies that don't value the importance of culture, which can result in a high turnover rate, disgruntled employees, and a lack of motivation.

Here are five signs that your company may need a cultural makeover.

1. A Lack of Patience

Building something great takes a lot of time, especially if you are working to solve a big problem that impacts a lot of people. Success does not come overnight, and you need to appreciate that the journey is the reward. You are going to have ups and downs, wins and losses, good days and bad days.

When people start to lack patience, they begin to make short-sighted decisions. Long-term strategies take a backseat to short-term problem solving as people lose sight of the big picture. When a lack of patience emerges, people tend to lose perspective and focus, which are vital ingredients for both business and cultural success.

When you can maintain a culture that understands this, you will see people exhibit the patience needed to ride out the tough times, as well as stay grounded during the high times.

2. Silos

For a company to succeed, silos must be removed so information and ideas are able to flow freely. Information is a powerful weapon at every level of the company.

Are people working on the right things at the right time? Are people aware of any strategic shifts that may impact their day-to-day priorities? Are people clear on how their work impacts others? When people can share without barriers, you create a sense of empowerment and collaboration that puts the company above individual business units and teams above self.

When you start to see silos form, tear them down. If people are starting to form cliques, change the office setup so people are not lumped together on their own islands. Publicly acknowledge and celebrate shared goals. Encourage cross-company mentoring and networking so people have exposure to other parts of the business. More than anything, give people a forum so they can understand how their work impacts the success of others and see everyone can help everyone else.

3. A Lack of Empathy

One of my favorite core values, and something I always look for in the people I work with (and for) is empathy. When people genuinely care about those around them and take a keen interest in making them better, the entire business benefits.

When you start to see people act in a way that compromises empathy, you will begin to see your culture fray. Accountability becomes an issue. People are more likely to blame others than help them. Kindness starts to become an absentee value, and people don't feel like they can rely on others. When teammates start to feel like they cannot rely on others, you are no longer getting the best out of your teams. Empathy is the catalyst for world class teamwork. Don't overlook it.

4. More Managers and Fewer Leaders

As a business grows, it is inevitable that more people will be put in positions of management. People who have excelled at whatever task they are responsible for are generally a great model for others to follow and learn from. If someone is succeeding, how can their acumen and style be passed on to others? In addition, management positions can be used as an incentive for motivating high flyers and people who are looking to grow their skills.

But management is different than leadership. When you start to have more managers than leaders, you start to lose cultural balance. Leaders can solve day-to-day problems, but they also set the tone for what is acceptable behavior through their actions. Leaders keep people motivated, grounded, inspired, and engaged. They correct bad behaviors that start to emerge within the team. When people are being managed vs. led, you'll see productivity decrease.

5. A Decrease in Engagement

Employee engagement is a vital part of a company's culture. It comes from everyone being on the same page, understanding the mission of the company, and knowing how they can contribute through the work they do. Great companies also give people tools to be engaged. Whether it is through all-hands meetings or technology that allows people to share feedback in real time (at Porch, we use TinyPulse), an engaged employee is one that helps make the culture great through their interactions and overall interest in every facet of the business.

When a company does not create a platform for people to be engaged, a job starts to feel like . . . well, a job. Employees don't feel valuable. They don't feel like they can go to anyone with concerns. They don't feel like they have a voice. When employees start to feel like they are just a cog in the wheel, it will show in the company's results. Not only will their sense of fulfillment and overall satisfaction dwindle, the business will suffer as distractions, worry, and uncertainty ultimately lead to a lack of productivity.

Watch for these signs to stay ahead of bad habits becoming the norm.

BURNOUT IS KILLING YOUR GROWTH

Mark Robinson

As entrepreneurs, many of us wear a badge of honor of our hard-charging work ethic and commitment—at all costs—to the success of the business. We're prouder still of our team members who display such dedication and relentlessly go the extra mile, especially those without significant incentives, like equity in the company. As with so many other things in life, you can definitely have too much of a good thing. Too many entrepreneurs don't understand how burned out their employees are.

According to a Workforce Institute study, 95 percent of HR professionals think that employee burnout is sabotaging a workforce's productivity. In contrast, a recent 2017 study we conducted showed that a third of employees felt burnt out, but over 49 percent of employees felt their managers had no idea about the extra time they put into their work. Most business leaders don't realize they have a problem, let alone seek to understand why it's happening.

What's more, the argument that burnt out employees are less productive doesn't seem to change hearts or minds of employers who see overworking employees as a necessary evil in order to remain competitive.

This might make them sit up and think: The poor management practices that foster a culture of employee burnout also have significant potential ramifications in restricting business growth. Here are three key reasons why this happens—and what you should do about it.

1. A Sample of One

As leaders, we're keen on making data-driven decisions. Our industry experience, heightened drive, and ability to process and apply data allow us to get tasks done efficiently. Data and the associated automation increasingly help to inform and action almost every decision made—from pricing to payables to promotions—with one important exception: people.

When it comes to managing employees' time, we typically base decisions on experience and gut instinct--not data. That's because as experienced business people, we make assessments on how long certain deliverables should take based on a sample size of one: ourselves. Entrepreneurs often don't record or analyze people's time to anywhere near the degree they should, leading to unrealistic expectations.

The impact here is that flawed assumptions on what the business can deliver and by when persist in all business planning. Finally, you reach a certain terminal velocity that you just can't break out of. Growth stalls.

To mitigate unrealistic expectations, business owners should collect and review actual data on how long each individual employee spends on every task. By gathering and reviewing data on how tasks are accomplished, leaders have more knowledgeable insight into the ways their employees work and how resources are allocated.

This data will allow for informed decisions about workloads but also give leaders opportunities to share their expertise with employees. Using data helps to plan resources so that employees don't feel as though they are set up to fail, overworking to get tasks done and perpetuating a cycle of unrealistic expectations which culminates in the business getting stuck in neutral (or worse).

2. Hidden Burnout

Business leaders are often timid about monitoring the overall picture of an individual employee's workload for fear of "micro-managing." However, you are likely doing a disservice to your team members when not getting a full picture of how much blood, sweat, and tears they are giving to the cause!

Overworked employees have a direct, negative effect on a business' ability to scale and grow. Managers should be to blame for this. Lack of visibility into the day-to-day workload of your employees is a poor management practice that wears out employees and can ultimately cripple the business.

It should also be done with a softer approach in tandem. Weekly, in-person debriefs with employees are a great way to detect whether they are saddled with too much and how it's affecting them individually.

Too many business leaders have no idea how much they are pushing their employees. That presents a challenge in maintaining growth and preventing a talent mass exodus. While having employees that understand the value of hard work and dedication is key for driving a successful business, especially in professional industries, having employees that are continuously burnt-out ultimately affects their personal productivity and the productivity of the business itself.

3. Feedback Dismissed

Whether it's your senior leadership team or the summer intern, entrepreneurs shouldn't be dismissive of feedback from anyone—especially feedback related to certain projects, clients, or tasks. As founders, we don't always understand the day-to-day happenings of our employees. By taking feedback and learning from it, we can better align our expectations. Implementing feedback also provides a level of transparency that benefits employees in allowing them to see firsthand the value they are bringing to the business.

Find a specific project every month or quarter to evaluate with your employees and ask for feedback. This technique shows employees that you are open to this type of dialogue to improve processes. Using feedback to adjust the scope of future projects is not only beneficial to employees but to the business's bottom line.

It can be gratifying that your team works hard as they go the extra mile for you and your business. But don't reward good work with more work. Watch for signs of burnout, and make sure you don't lose your best and brightest.

WHEN YOU TAKE CULTURE TOO FAR

Jayson DeMers

If you've been plugged into the entrepreneurial world at all in the past decade or so, you've probably heard people describe how they want all their employees to "live and breathe" the company culture. The metaphor here is designed to imply a commitment to that culture—usually defined as its values, character, and priorities—so deep that it can no longer be distinguished from the employees' own individual values, character, and priorities.

It's an interesting perspective that certainly has its merits: when all your employees are so deeply committed to the company, they'll be willing to work harder for their shared goals and more likely to work together. They'll also contribute more positively to the overall environment, creating an accelerating feedback loop that makes the culture even stronger.

However, a live-and-breathe type of culture takes the idea to an extreme that yields more than a handful of downsides. And really, the only reason the concept even exists is because of our (hopefully temporary) obsession with the importance of company culture.

The Rise of Company Culture

Organizational culture has been a concept in business and management since at least the 1970s, but it's only recently that "corporate culture" has become a buzzword. You could argue that this is because more business leaders are discovering the objective value of a positive company culture. I'd argue, however, that it's something closer to a fad.

Company culture started to accelerate in popularity once people started realizing that many tech startups in the Silicon Valley region that eventually turned into multibillion-dollar juggernauts all had surprising cultural features in common that broke from traditional office environments.

Obscure furniture, casual dress codes, and a youthful energy were and still are stereotypically common features in this context. However, they fuel a false correlation: Both financial success and culture differentiate these companies, so surely the two factors must be connected.

The end result is a still-growing obsession with creating a unique and "modern" corporate culture—one that employees must live and breathe to allow for that culture's full benefits.

When Culture Goes Too Far

This illustration shouldn't convince you that corporate culture is bad or unnecessary. In fact, I argue that it's critical for business success. But we should be careful not to overestimate culture's benefits and avoid shoving it down workers' throats.

Let's look at the disadvantages of company culture gone too far:

- *Homogeneity.* Some of the best ideas in the world are the ones you didn't see coming. They come from outside sources and perspectives or arise from uncomfortable situations. Accordingly, having a diverse environment with many different minds and perspectives is important to a business's survival. Being too rigid and too serious about your company culture encourages a kind of homogeneity. If all your employees think and act alike, they'll all solve problems the same way, which will limit your growth and put you at risk for bigger problems down the road.

- *Stress and pressure.* Using the phrase "living and breathing" company culture implies that working for this company is as important as life itself. While some people thrive in high-pressure environments, chronic stress isn't good for anybody. If you make your workers feel like nothing matters except their work, eventually they will begin to suffer lower morale and display lowered productivity.

- *Polarization.* Approaching company culture with this extreme level will also polarize your newest hires and job candidates. It's true that you'll naturally attract some people who already fall in line with your company values, but you'll also scare away some serious talent who may differ with you on a handful of key points. Is that scenario really worth it?

- *Misplaced values.* Don't forget: this is still a business, and your bottom line is profitability.

Company culture is a useful way to make your workers happier and more productive, but the "living and breathing" angle can sometimes interfere with that vision. For example, if an employee's deviation from your cultural norms ends up earning better results for your business, you shouldn't complain or reprimand the employee.

- *Cult vibes.* Finally, to a more subjective point: enforcing your company culture too strictly or seriously gives off some serious cult vibes. This is off-putting to employees, clients, and customers alike. Try not to turn your brand into a corporate brainwashing scheme.

Find the Right Balance

Remember, company culture is still important and your employees should, to some degree, fit into that culture. The key is to find the balance between nurturing that culture and mandating it. It's different for every business; depending on your size, your niche, and your personal preferences, you may end up settling on one end of the spectrum or the other. There isn't a single right answer, but you owe it to your staff and the future of your business to give it some serious thought.

ENTREPRENEUR VOICES SPOTLIGHT: INTERVIEW WITH MIKEY TRAFTON

Founder of Blue Fish

When Everyone Quit on the Same Day

In his interview at the end of Part II, Jason Cohen referenced a "dramatic" story that sparked a paradigmatic shift in his whole view on organizational culture.

This is that story.

Entrepreneur: Mikey, tell us your tale of woe.

Trafton: Twenty years ago, I founded Blue Fish Development Group to create the company where I wanted to work. I'd worked in other places and didn't like how they prioritized some aspects of the business and didn't prioritize others, especially when those things were in the best interests of our clients.

My first big client was a tech company in Silicon Valley building their corporate website. The project was so big that I needed to hire seven people to deliver it. As an individual contributor, I'd never managed or hired people before. I had no idea what I was doing. I knew how to build the technology and manage a project, but running a company was something else.

I had a buddy I'd worked with in a previous job and convinced him to come work for me. When I told him I needed six more people, he said, "You know what? I just happen to know six people who would be great for the job. We've all worked together in past companies and we all get along super well together." All eight of us had lunch over fajitas and without interviewing them or doing anything else, idiot that I was, I decided to hire them. We got to work immediately.

In the first three months, we made $300,000. Everything was going right. We were living the dream. The next three months, we lost $300,000, and the project went off the rails.

I started tightening down the screws and micromanaging everyone. I pushed them to deliver. I told them they weren't getting their projects done on time or that the quality wasn't good. I hired testers to double check all their code. I hired a project manager to keep everyone on track. I created a little website where everyone had to log in all their tasks and the time it took. I just kept pushing and pushing and pushing.

One of the main problems was that all of them had come from large corporate backgrounds where deadlines got pushed back all the time. I came from a consulting role where deadlines were guaranteed by contract; that date drove everything else. We came from two fundamentally different, mismatched perspectives.

In another effort to force them to work harder, I leased office space in downtown Denver and made them all come to work in a central location, where before they had all been working from home. It didn't help. Things still weren't improving. It just made me try to drive everyone that much harder.

Then one day, I got an email from one of them: he quit. Twenty minutes later, I got an email from another guy: he quit. Then another. By the end of the day, the entire company had quit.

Entrepreneur: Your entire company quit in one day. That's every business owner's nightmare.

Trafton: This nuclear bomb had gone off in my world. Of course, I was still on the hook for my contract with my client. I still had the lease on the office space. I still had to deliver and pay the bills.

A couple of them said, "Look, we know that you still need to get this done. We quit, but you can hire us back as freelancers." I was forced to—at triple the rate I'd been paying them before. I survived, obviously, but it was one of the worst experiences of my career.

Entrepreneur: Now that the years have passed, what's your take on that whole experience?

Trafton: As I said, we were fundamentally mismatched. They wanted to operate the company more like a commune: everybody decides what part of the project they want, how many hours they want to put into it, and what projects to take on in the first place. So they went off and formed their own company. And you know what? They did great. They were happy, and they were in business for years.

But I had a more deliberate approach to business. I wanted to organize the resources and efforts the way I thought best. Meeting deadlines and honoring our commitments was important to me, so I wanted to do whatever it took to achieve that.

Once we parted ways, I was happier, too. It was like a bad marriage. It's not often that one party is just a bad person—it's just not a good match.

Entrepreneur: How did you go about rebuilding Blue Fish?

Trafton: You know, it's not every entrepreneur who has the "luxury" of having the entire company quit in one day. It was like wiping the slate clean. I got to start over from scratch.

This time, I was more intentional about who I hired. I needed people who saw business the way I did and who wanted to work the way I did. I really do love going the extra mile for my clients, even when it's not the most prudent thing financially. We have a saying at Blue Fish: "You're a culture fit if you do more for others than you do for yourself." That means that I shouldn't hire someone who's self-centered. Making a bit of self-sacrifice goes against what they are. Again, that doesn't make them bad people, but it means that they probably don't want to serve the client the way I do.

In fact, you want to keep those kind of bad culture fits away from you altogether. I tell entrepreneurs, "Fly your freak flag high!" Tell potential employees what you're all about—the more eccentric, the better. You want them to see you from afar, and the people who are attracted to those qualities will run to you; the people who don't like it will run the other way.

The Army used to have a commercial that said, "We do more before 9 A.M. than most people do all day." I look at that and say, "That sounds terrible! I don't want anything to do with that!" But there are plenty of people who love that. That message repels me but attracts them.

Entrepreneur: So you flew your freak flag high and… attracted a bunch of freaks?

Trafton: I found a lot of people who like to do business the way I like to do business. They're a wonderful team that puts the client first. In fact, we won an award for being the best place to work in Austin. From the company that everybody quit to the company where everybody loves to work.

Entrepreneur: And everyone lived happily ever after.

Trafton: No—then the financial crisis hit and we lost nearly all of our accounts. The big companies pulled back on their spending for tech consulting. It was awful.

We have an open-book policy at our company, so people saw what was coming. They saw our cash reserves dwindling. They knew it was dire.

I called a company-wide meeting and said, "Look, we've got to make some cuts. We're probably going to have to lay a bunch of you off. If some of you are willing to take a pay cut or something, we may be able to hold off on that a little bit longer. But as it stands, we're going to be doing layoffs soon."

That was tough. That was me having to stand in front of my team and basically tell them that I was a failure. As the CEO, I hadn't done my job. I hadn't been back in my office very long when one of our sales guys came in and said, "Mikey, I'll tell you what. Just pay me my salary. You don't have to pay me my commissions for the next few months until we get this settled and this blows over."

He left and another guy came in: "You know, I've been meaning to take some time off and travel with my boyfriend. You don't have to pay my salary for the next three months if you'll just cover my health insurance."

As soon as he walked out, someone else walked in: "Hey, you can cut my salary by 20 percent, okay?"

Someone else: "Look, I can take a 10 percent cut." By the end of the day, everyone had come into my office and offered to make some sort of financial sacrifice. Every. Single. Person.

Entrepreneur: Same owner—same company, even—same "company is facing difficulty" scenario, and yet two diametrically opposite reactions.

Trafton: It was the greatest moment of my professional life. Everyone sacrificed something to stay together as long as we could, and not because they couldn't find jobs elsewhere. We had rock stars. Even in the recession, their skills were in high demand. They didn't have to make that financial sacrifice. They could have replaced their income by just walking across the street. But they sacrificed because they loved each other and wanted to stay together.

That's the power of culture.

PART IV
DYSFUNCTION—REFLECTIONS

While this section does seem the most negative, in an odd way, it's also the most hopeful. These are largely stories about companies and entrepreneurs who got it wrong, and yet still found a way to overcome. These are examples of triumph—not over the market or over the naysayers, but over the self.

As we noted earlier, especially in the section on leadership, culture begins with you, the entrepreneur. Leading change in culture begins with changing yourself.

The interview with the founder of Blue Fish is one of the best illustrations of just how fundamental this idea is. The only difference between everyone quitting and everyone sacrificing to stay together was the entrepreneur's focus on culture.

It's not that he changed, per se; he changed his approach.

That's really the takeaway from this section. By the time you're an adult, who and what you are is largely set. Nature and nurture and all that. It's extraordinarily difficult to change our habits, our thinking, and our worldview. But it's comparatively easy to get intentional about some things you may have taken for granted.

When you reflect on the advice in this book, that's the underlying point. These mavens of company culture didn't have neurosurgery to rewire their thinking—they simply focused on what was important and got serious about making sure they keep their priorities straight.

When they took care of the foundation, success took care of itself.

RESOURCES

(In Order of Appearance)

Thank you to our talented Entrepreneur contributors whose content is featured in this book. For more information about these contributors, including author bios, visit us at www.entrepreneur.com.

1. Sara Sutton Fell, "How a Business With No Office Has One of the Best Company Cultures in America," *Entrepreneur*, March 22, 2017, www.entrepreneur.com/article/290172.

2. Jeremy Swift, "What Switching to Lyft Taught Me About Tech's Authenticity Problem," *Entrepreneur*, August 15, 2017, www.entrepreneur.com/article/297832.

3. Matt Mayberry, "Want to Be Like Apple, Disney or the New England Patriots? You Need a Stellar Company Culture," *Entrepreneur*, March 4, 2017, www.entrepreneur.com/article/271900.

4. Ben Judah, "How Your Culture Will Ensure You Keep Your Edge," *Entrepreneur*, April 10, 2017, www.entrepreneur.com/article/290829.

5. Steffen Maier, "5 Companies Getting Employee Engagement Right," *Entrepreneur*, December 28, 2016, www.entrepreneur.com/article/285052.

6. Robert Wallace, "A Set of Core Values Is What Makes Company Culture a Real Thing," *Entrepreneur*, July 28, 2017, www.entrepreneur.com/article/279186.

7. Brian Patrick Eha, "How Your Leadership Skills Will Determine Your Company Culture," *Entrepreneur*, March 21, 2017, www.entrepreneur.com/article/270488.

8. Rose Leadem, "This Founder and CEO of a Unicorn Has a 'No Shoes' Policy," *Entrepreneur*, July 11, 2017, www.entrepreneur.com/article/296971.

9. Tony Delmercado, "3 Key Steps to Expand Your Culture to New Cities," *Entrepreneur*, February 20, 2017, www.entrepreneur.com/article/289368.

10. Pratik Dholakiya, "4 Foundational Tips for Creating a Viable Company Culture," *Entrepreneur*, May 23, 2017, www.entrepreneur.com/article/294588.

11. Tony Delmercado, "Which Came First: Culture or Growth? Hopefully, It's Culture," *Entrepreneur*, June 3, 2017, www.entrepreneur.com/article/276225.

12. Anka Wittenberg, "3 Ways to Simplify Your Company Culture and Build Trust," *Entrepreneur*, May 2, 2017, www.entrepreneur.com/article/272148.

13. Jeffrey Hayzlett, "6 Steps to Building a Strong Company Culture," *Entrepreneur*, June 22, 2017, www.entrepreneur.com/article/277727.

14. Peter Daisyme, "Creating a Company Culture Where Employees Never Leave," *Entrepreneur*,

April 7, 2015, www.entrepreneur.com/article/243134.

15. Nadya Khoja, "A CEO's Main Focus Should Be Improving Company Culture," *Entrepreneur*, April 5, 2017, www.entrepreneur.com/article/290296.

16. John Rampton, "Do Raises Make Employees Happy or Is It Something More?" *Entrepreneur*, July 18, 2017, www.entrepreneur.com/article/297326.

17. Kelly Lovell, "5 Ways to Foster Team Culture on a Startup Budget," *Entrepreneur*, January 4, 2017, www.entrepreneur.com/article/254057.

18. Heather R. Huhman, "This is How Your Employees Really See Your Company Culture," *Entrepreneur*, August 29, 2017, www.entrepreneur.com/article/281065.

19. Steffen Maier, "How Google Uses People Analytics to Create a Great Workplace," *Entrepreneur*, November 28, 2016, www.entrepreneur.com/article/284550.

20. Sujan Patel, "The Secret to Creating a Great Company Culture: Open Communication and Feedback," *Entrepreneur*, December 12, 2016, www.entrepreneur.com/article/284368.

21. Peter Daisyme, "Fun, Flexibility and Competition Will Put the Pep Back in the Step of Your Staff," *Entrepreneur*, March 18, 2017, www.entrepreneur.com/article/272530.

22. Andrew Medal, "Why Wellness Should Be on Your Company Culture Checklist," *Entrepreneur,* March 10, 2017, www.entrepreneur.com/article/290114.

23. Shellye Archambeau, "3 Strategies for CEOs to Improve Corporate Culture," *Entrepreneur*, June 5, 2017, www.entrepreneur.com/article/295171.

24. Nina Zipkin, "Uber Needs to Recreate its Company Culture. Here's What You Can Learn From Its Mistakes," *Entrepreneur*, June 15, 2017, www.entrepreneur.com/article/295844.

25. Ray Hennessey, "What a 'Best Butt' Award Says About Bad Corporate Culture," *Entrepreneur*, June 21, 2017, www.entrepreneur.com/article/277798.

26. Rob Villeneuve, "5 Ways to Turn Your Company Culture Around," *Entrepreneur*, July 18, 2017, www.entrepreneur.com/article/278988.

27. Matthew Baker, "Here's the Secret to Improving Employee Engagement That Every Company Can Afford," *Entrepreneur*, June 13, 2017, www.entrepreneur.com/article/294634.

28. Ray Hennessey, "Good Company Culture Is Not About Silly, Attention-Grabbing Perks," *Entrepreneur*, June 1, 2017, www.entrepreneur.com/article/276679.

29. Travis Bradberry, "8 Ways Cutthroat Work Cultures Suck the Life Out of You," *Entrepreneur*, November 1, 2016, www.entrepreneur.com/article/284385.

30. Craig Cincotta, "5 Signs Your Corporate Culture is Doomed," *Entrepreneur*, August 21, 2015, www.entrepreneur.com/article/249778.

31. Mark Robinson, "Do You Even Realize How Your Burnout Culture Is Hampering Your Growth?" *Entrepreneur*, August 16, 2017, www.entrepreneur.com/article/295873.

32. Jayson DeMers, "Why a 'Living and Breathing' Company Culture Isn't Always a Good Thing," *Entrepreneur*, April 3, 2017, www.entrepreneur.com/article/292095.

Reader's Notes

Reader's Notes

_____

_____

_____

_____

_____

_____

_____

_____

_____

_____

_____

_____

_____

_____

_____

_____

_____

_____

Reader's Notes

_____

_____

_____

_____

_____

_____

_____

_____

_____

_____

_____

_____

_____

_____

_____

_____

_____

_____

_____

_____

Reader's Notes